Sport

In memory of Jenny

Sport

Social problems and issues

Frank Kew

Butterworth-Heinemann
Linacre House, Jordan Hill, Oxford OX2 8DP
225 Wildwood Avenue, Woburn, MA 01801-2041
A division of Reed Educational and Professional Publishing Ltd

ℛ A member of the Reed Elsevier plc group

OXFORD   AUCKLAND   BOSTON
JOHANNESBURG   MELBOURNE   NEW DELHI

First published 1997
Reprinted 1998, 2000

British Library Cataloguing in Publication Data
A catalogue record for this book is available from the British Library

ISBN 0 7506 2892 8

Typeset by David Gregson Associates, Beccles, Suffolk
Printed and bound in Great Britain by Biddles Ltd
www.biddles.co.uk

PLANT A TREE

BTCV
British Trust for
Conservation Volunteers

FOR EVERY TITLE THAT WE PUBLISH, BUTTERWORTH-HEINEMANN
WILL PAY FOR BTCV TO PLANT AND CARE FOR A TREE.

Contents

Foreword   vii

Preface   ix

Part One   Sport as Social Practice and
***   Social Institution***   1
1 Sport: inside out   5
Look at it this way   5
Sport as a social practice   8
Sport as a socal institution   11
A delicate balancing act   14

2 Sports: change and development   15
Characteristics of modern sports   15
Changes to sports processes   19
Changes to sport worlds   22
Different sports, different problems   27
A critical note   31

3 Sports in the marketplace   32
Introduction   32
Sport and capital   33
Sponsorship   36
The sponsorship–advertizing–media axis   40
Globalization   49
Some key questions   51

4 The corruption of sports practice   56
Introduction   56
Types of disassociation: contest problems   59
Typical response to contest problems   63
Types of disassociation: pre-contest problems   67
The exploitation and abuse of athletes   68
Responses to exploitation   75
Codes of conduct for coaches   77
A critical note: individual or system   77

Part Two Sport and Structural Inequality   83

5 Sport, racism and ethnicity   87
Multiculturalism   87
Racism   89
The Afro-Caribbean experience   92
South Asians and sport   101

6 Sport, ability and disability   108
Introduction   108
Society disables   108
The accessibility of sports   111
Integration   118
Competitive sport   119
Different but equitable   122

7 Sport and gender   124
What's the problem   124
Sex, gender and sexism   126
Gender relations   127
Who rules, who coaches?   135
Strategies for equity   137

8 Sport and social class   143
Introduction: the end of the class   143
Social surveys   144
Dimension of class   148
The habitus   150
An underclass?   157
Class rules   158
Summary   159

References   161

Further reading   173

Index   177

Foreword

For many years, one of the problems facing anyone interested in how sport fits into British society has been the dearth of a readable text which deals predominantly with sport in Britain rather than sport in North America.

At last, Dr Frank Kew has provided a book which is rooted in British society and culture. No more Green Bay Packers and Vince Lombardi, step forward rugby league and Ellery Hanley. Most of us are touched by the sports world which Frank Kew reveals. Coaches, performers, officials, teachers and families will all be fascinated when they consider the sports world which surrounds them.

This text should serve as core reading for students of sport sociology but it provides more than an academic reference. Combining basic theoretical perspectives with practical examples, the book does not require a vast knowledge of sociology, just an enquiring mind about how society and sport interact in Britain.

This book will encourage you to reflect on where you are in the sports world, what are your views on topical issues such as the influence of satellite television or the effect of racism on sport. Most of all it will enlighten you and make you think.

David Houlston
Head of Education and Training
The National Coaching Foundation
Headingley, Leeds

Preface

Most readers of this book will have an active interest in sport, will have, or be anticipating, a career related to sports, or be both an accomplished performer and a knowledgeable consumer. We take sport seriously in our society. Individuals invest heavily in sport in terms of time, energy, money and emotional commitment, either as participants or spectators. Because sports are a significant element of popular culture, commercial and political organizations also invest heavily in its practice from recreational to elite levels. In short, a **value** is placed on sport – by individuals, by the state, by business – and anything which threatens to compromise, undermine or restrict its practice excites interest and critical comment.

Consequently, many of the issues discussed here are already in the public domain – in journalistic commentary on sport, in specialist sports magazines, in the policy-making and strategic organization of both the public and voluntary sectors of sports provision and, indeed, in the everyday informal conversation of social and sporting-interest groups.

The purpose of this book is to provide an accessible and balanced account of some of the main developments in modern sport and the problems and issues which confront practitioners, whether as players, organizers, coaches, teachers, providers or administrators of sport. Most of the problems and social issues discussed here, however, are not exclusively the domain of sports, but rather they relate to the kind of society we live in, the broader social, economic and political dynamics from which sports derive their significance.

The book is organized into two parts which have a different focus. Part One focuses primarily but not exclusively upon issues deriving from sports

performance, whereas Part Two is principally concerned with the **accessibility** of sports. After some preliminary observations about the nature and development of modern sports, Part One considers the complex ways in which sports are increasingly being governed by a market rationality, where the interests of commerce and the media are becoming more significant, for players, for sports clubs and for governing bodies. Not only are sports exploited by business, but the increasing seriousness and competitiveness of sports leads to a range of corrupt practices such as cheating, player violence, athlete-abuse and drug-taking.

Part Two draws upon critical perspectives about sport and the reproduction of structural inequality, to examine the continued inequity in opportunities for sports, and the policy responses of the public and voluntary sectors of sports provision. Dimensions of inequity are examined with reference to race and ethnicity, gender, social class and disability.

This is not intended as an apologia, but given the scope of this book, the treatment of social issues in sports can only be at an introductory level and, via the reference material, the reader is guided towards the more specialist literature on the main themes. I have tried to organize and present some of the current critical debates about the nature and practice of modern sports which, I hope, will contribute to enhancing its practice. Sports are undergoing rapid change and development, processes which need to be carefully managed – by readers of this book among others.

Frank Kew
Ilkley

Part One

Sport as Social Practice and Social Institution

Here are some extracts of an article about British sport by Howard Marshall, a former Oxford Rugby Blue, writing in *The Listener*:

> Sport should be guided by honour and sanctioned by fair play ... the growth of the competitive element minimises our proper enjoyment of games and sports.

> Village cricket is one of the few games which still have the spontaneous vitality, fun, and happiness which I should like to see everywhere.

> Games and relaxation have their proper place in the scheme of things; but when one particular game monopolises a man's entire energies, it ceases to be a game and becomes an obsession or a somewhat useless part-time job.

> Let us admit right away that a game like rugby is an influence for the good. ... The game spreads good fellowship, hardiness, and courage ... it sweats the vice out of a man.

> ... our growing love of the spectacular is blinding us to the true purpose of games and sports.

> All we can do is to hold fast to what virtues remain in sport, and spread as widely as possible the true principles of games-playing, and hope for ... a gradual return to a rational scale of values.

These extracts contain a number of assumptions and value-judgements about sports participation. First, sports are a good thing if they are played at rather than worked at, and if the player upholds and respects the values of fair play and sportsmanship. Secondly, sports are a good thing because they enable people to direct their energies towards socially acceptable and wholesome pursuits, and away from antisocial and even criminal activity. Thirdly, sports are becoming too serious, too competitive, with too much emphasis on spectacle, a development which undermines and endangers the intrinsic qualities of sport.

The more astute reader will have gathered, through the somewhat arcane and sexist language, that these extracts are not a contemporary piece of writing. Marshall wrote his 'inquisition' on British sport in 1931, seven years before the publication of the influential text *Homo Ludens* (Man at Play), in which Huizinga (a Dutchman) bemoaned the bastardization of the 'sacred realm' of play by the 'profane spectacle' of modern sports. Similarly, Stone (1970), in an article entitled 'American sports: play and display', provided a critical commentary on the putative loss of playfulness in contemporary sports and its transformation into 'display' (meaning spectacle) and 'dis-play' (meaning un-playful).

Each of these writers, in different national contexts, were addressing social problems and issues which, at the time, they saw as threatening the integrity of sports, and the experiences and challenges these diverse activities provide for participants. The writings span the decades either side of the Second World War. Marshall was writing before the invention of television, but in an era witnessing a massive growth in sports spectatorship. Huizinga's text was published two years after the first overt and deliberate manipulation of sport for political ends (the Berlin Olympics). Stone was recognizing the growing 'spectacularization' of sports events in the USA in the mid-1950s, consequent upon the increasing influence of television, and the growing realization by commercial entrepreneurs that profit was to be made from sports.

Each of these writers, in their different ways, is critical of these developments and, at least, implicitly adhere to an idealized image of 'true' (i.e. playful, fun) sports being undermined by the changing social, economic and technological contexts within which they are practised. The kernel of these debates remains the subject of much critical social commentary today. The most radical commentators argue that modern sport is so debased that salvage is impossible (e.g. Brohm, 1978; Rigauer, 1981; Eichberg, 1984), and that we need a wholesale revisioning and re-evaluation of the realm of play and recreation.

This text adopts a more lenient view to argue that (a) sports are worth preserving and developing, but (b) rather than resisting change, and celebrating and fostering, in myth rather than fact, an image of a bygone sunlit Arcadia where players played in an unsullied and bucolic state, the task for sports practitioners is to be proactive in both embracing and managing changes to ensure the integrity of sporting challenges for the future.

The opening two chapters of Part One provide a basis for the subsequent analysis of social problems and issues. Chapter 1 locates and examines the source of most contemporary problems and issues in sport as an **inescapable** and irreducible tension or dynamic between sports as conceived as a range of **social practices** and sports as a **social institution**. The second chapter adopts an historical and developmental perspective to examine change both to the social practice of sport and the institutional arrangements of its practice. Together, these provide a framework for considering the burgeoning influence of commerce on sport, and the pressures which lead to cheating, violence and other practices which corrupt sport.

Sport: inside out

chapter one

Look at it this way!

> The paradox of sport is that it provides such moments (of self realization) even as it confirms their apparent impossibility elsewhere. It both realizes human identity and denies other kinds of (especially racial and sexual) identity. It is both uncontaminated by the rest of social life and shot through with economic and political influences. It is both timeless and a product of history (Critcher, 1984).

Many of the current debates about social problems in sport articulate around the two different perspectives on sport encapsulated in the above observation. The artistic term 'perspective' suggests that one gets a different view of an object relative to one's position or distance from that object. The same applies to sport – writers adopt different theoretical positions and/or write from positions of involvement in, or detachment from, sporting practice. Consider the following two statements:

> Play is essentially a free activity quite consciously outside 'ordinary' life as being 'not serious', but at the same time absorbing the player intensely and utterly. Play has no material interest, and no profit can be gained by it. It proceeds within its own proper boundaries of time and space according to fixed rules and in an orderly manner. It promotes the formation of social groupings which tend to surround themselves with secrecy and to stress their differences from the common world by disguise or other means (Huizinga, 1972).

In Huizinga's eyes, his comments about the intrinsic qualities of play should apply equally well to sport; a sacred realm of activity set apart from other activities. In contrast, another perspective is as follows:

> ... sport is not a 'privileged space' into which we can retreat from real life – rather it is systematically and intimately connected with society. Sport as an activity, or an object of interest, is socially constructed; it is defined and given meaning. It is these meanings which give us the value of being involved in sport – they provide us with identities and identifications (Clarke and Clarke, 1982).

Two wholly different perspectives on sport. The first is that, through their specific rule structures, sports are distinctive social practices, self-contained, and separated out from the rest of social life. All sports (including those which take place in natural environments like climbing or canoeing) provide a set of psychomotor challenges, conditioned by rules, regulations and the necessary equipment, and for which participants have developed skills and strategies in order to meet that sporting challenge. This perspective brings into sharp relief the difference of sport to other activities, the nature and structures of a diverse range of sporting challenges which have been, and continue to be, developed. We can call this the 'time-out' perspective – the suspension of the ordinary, the entering into a separate sphere of social life.

The second perspective on sport is to consider the broader social context within and through which sports have changed and developed over time. Sports do not take place in a vacuum but rather are subsumed under the paramount reality of the social world, their meaning and significance deriving from the values which are placed on their practice by powerful interest groups outside sport, i.e. those groupings who are able to impose on others their evaluations of what counts as acceptable, useful and successful sporting practice.

Huizinga's perspective is dismissed by some as being both idealist and ahistorical. It is 'idealist' because, in stressing that 'the impulse to play' transcends historical epochs, he neglects or minimizes the social and economic conditions within which modern sports developed. It is 'ahistorical' because he fails to recognize that sports (unlike play forms) are a product of industrial society and the particular social and economic relationships brought about by capitalism. Others would argue that the second perspective is incomplete because there is little acknowledgement of the particularity of sporting practices, of the experiences they provide, or of their sustained appeal for generations of participants. Many sociologists of sport, with the notable exception of Elias and Dunning (1986) and Morgan (1984), neglect the constitutive features of sports to focus exclusively upon environing influences; the social context of their practice.

The analytical framework adopted here is to incorporate both perspectives and to consider sport as a 'duality' – as having a double nature, as having both an inside and outside, as being simultaneously set apart from, yet part of, the rest of social life. This framework is similar to that adopted by Haywood *et al.* (1995) in their account of the duality of play, its intrinsic and extrinsic dimensions. They write:

> One of the primary qualities of the experience of play is that it is 'disinterested'; it is activity for its own sake, for no ulterior interest.... On the other hand, play is often valued precisely because of the purposes it might fulfil, purposes which have little to do with the playing itself. This enables us to examine the ways in which the functional or purposeful meanings and goals ascribed to play are intimately related to, and dependent upon, play's intrinsic qualities.

Sport, however, is different from play in so far as it involves sedimented and standardized widespread practices. Therefore, and borrowing from both MacIntyre (1981) and Lasch (1979), the duality of sport will be analysed by conceiving sport as **both** a 'social practice' **and** as a 'social institution'. Understanding the distinction between social practice and social institution is important in making sense of, and coming to an informed assessment of, the social problems and issues in sports (Figure 1.1).

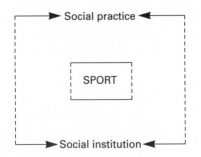

Figure 1.1 The duality of sport

Sport as a social practice

The social practice of sport is a **joint project** in which 'goods' or values internal to that project are realized in the course of trying to achieve the standards of excellence in it. These **internal goods** or values can only be achieved by engaging in the practice in question. Let us unpack this statement.

A joint project

A joint project means that people collaborate with each other, submit to the authority of rules, and agree to the contract to compete in order to bring about or actualize the social practice. A failure or refusal to engage in this collaborative enterprise is destructive of the social practice, and therefore of its internal goods or values. Instances of intentional rule-breaking, the use of performance-enhancing drugs, so-called 'professional' fouls, using banned technology which bestows an advantage, are all failures or refusals to abide by the contract of sport, i.e. being either a cheat or a spoilsport, either a hypocrite or a heretic (see Chapter 5).

The concept of sports as joint collaborative projects can be further analysed by considering the complex **social dynamics** involved in their practice. In this context, social dynamics refers to the ways in which the 'practitioners' (i.e. the participants or players) interact with one another. Elaborating on Luschen 1970), three sets of social dynamics are identified which apply to all forms of games and most other sports. These are:

- association (inter-group collaboration)
- cooperation (intra-group collaboration)
- competition

as shown in Figure 1.2.

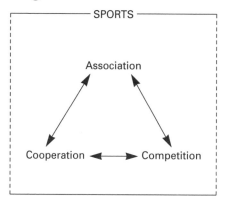

Figure 1.2 Social dynamics of sport

Association indicates collaboration **between** groups. All must collaborate in this way in order to put the activity (sport) into practice. All must enter into a contract to agree to join an internally and externally controlled system governed by rules. The Football 'Association' is a good example of this, where the groups are individual soccer clubs.

Cooperation indicates a form of collaboration where the rewards are shared **within** a group, team or squad. Individual members have to cooperate with one another in order to deploy their collective resources and therefore compete effectively. Most coaching is about mobilizing a group's collective resources, devising tactics and strategies based upon an assessment of the opposition's resources. Intra-group collaboration applies particularly to team games but also to any sports contests which are organized within group or squad frameworks.

Competition is the third and most commonly understood social dynamic and which clearly under-pins most spectators' interest in sport. Sports are meaningless unless the participants attempt to achieve goals and outcomes. Team games are mean-ingless unless players try to defend their own territory while attacking the opposing team's territory in order to score points, goals, etc. Competition against others, or oneself (e.g. personal bests), is a necessary but not a sufficient condition for all sports.

It is important to remember that these three sets of dynamics are **interdependent**, i.e. each gets its meaning from the other two, and it illustrates the complex social relations inherent in the social prac-tice of sport. A win-at-all costs attitude, instances of cheating and drug-use result in tipping the balance of social dynamics towards the interest in competition and away from an interest in association.

Internal goods

Internal goods or values are realized in the course of engaging in the joint collaborative project (i.e. the sport practice) and cannot, by definition, be achieved in any other way. Internal goods act as their own rewards for sports practitioners and might include:

- the exercise of skills
- the successful deployment of performance re-sources (e.g. devising successful tactics and strategies)
- testing and developing physical capabilities
- the experiences of exhilaration and of achievement, the rewards for the commitment and dedication that went into building the skills in the first place

- the qualities of social interaction with others engaged on the same project.[1]

Many writers, such as Novak (1976), Arnold (1979), Pearson (1979), Allen and Fahey (1982), Kleinman (1982) and Ravizza (1982) attempt to describe the rich experiential dimensions of sports participation. In similar vein, albeit with more empirical precision, Csikszentmihalyi (1975, 1992) attests to the 'flow' experience to be had by participants if one structures and values the sporting activity appropriately. In a survey of rock-climbers, basketball players, chess players and musicians, he found that most were intrinsically motivated, i.e. valuing the internal goods over the external goods of the practice. For Csikszentmihalyi, internal goods, encapsulated in his extensive analysis of the 'flow' experience, include:

- enjoyment of the experience and the use of skill
- the activity itself, the pattern, the action and the 'world' it provides with unambiguous feedback
- attention is focused on a limited stimulus field, on the process of doing rather than the outcomes
- a merging of action and awareness, complete absorption, a loss of consciousness of self, a sense of control.

Sport as a social institution

Some sociologists see institutions as fulfilling the 'needs' of individuals; others focus upon the ways in which people create or adapt to institutions rather than merely respond to them. Nevertheless, the term is widely used to describe 'social practices that are regularly and continuously repeated, are sanctioned and maintained by social norms, and have a major

[1] A full account of the internal goods of sports, and a philosophical defence of amateurism, is provided by Schneider and Butcher (1993).

significance in the social structure' (Abercrombie, 1984).

Social practices such as sports, require institutions for their very survival. Rugby or hockey, for example, require people in clubs, schools and associations, to develop an organizational and administrative system in order to sustain and develop the social practice. In part, the rationale for developing these systems is linked to a belief in the educational and socializing qualities of the experiences which the social practices of sport provide. However, unlike social practices in which goods **internal** to that project are realized, social institutions are *necessarily* concerned with the acquisition and distribution of **external** goods. Schneider and Butcher (1993) point out that, unlike internal goods, external goods such as wealth and fame are common currency, and can be achieved in a multiplicity of ways – their value is clear and clearly shared.

At an individual level, external goods might include the status, prestige, power and financial rewards which accrue from successful performance. At a supra-individual level, sports are promoted and developed by schools, by industry, by the local and national state, because they are seen to transmit social values deemed to be worthwhile by the larger society, such as achievement, discipline, teamwork, mental and physical fitness, health and good character. For example, a whole industry has developed on the, often implicit, assumption that outdoor pursuits build character and promote team-work. Compare these 'goods' with the internal goods listed earlier.

Social institutions implicitly underwrite and legiti-mize external goals and they act to encourage the social practitioner (i.e. the player, coach or manager) to value the internal goods of the sport **only** in so far as they realize external goals. This point about the duality of sport is recognized by Lasch (1979):

> Practices have to be sustained by institutions which in the very nature of things, tend to corrupt the practices they sustain.

This is the kernel of the issues discussed in the first part of the book. In mainstream sports organizations, the central problem is to protect and enhance the integrity of sports practice in the face of institutional pressures which threaten to prostitute sports in the interests of gaining external rewards. For others, however, the issue is even more fundamental, leading to a radical revisioning of modern sports, at both the level of social practice and institution, to establish a more inclusive, humanistic and non-alienating sphere of play.

Feminist scholarship makes an important contribution to radical reassessments of sporting values, as is noted in Chapter 7. Nelson (1991), for example, proposes two models for understanding sport.[2] The first is the 'military model' or pinnacle-of-success model, the second is the 'partnership' or non-hierarchical model. The first is characterized as having an overwhelming concern with rankings, authoritarian relationships between coaches and players, highly competitive relationships between competitors, a constant search for improved performance, and an overwhelming interest in who won. Most people have been socialized into and accept this model of sport. The second model sees sport as 'inclusive, in balance with other aspects of life, educational in orientation, and co-operative and social in spirit'. This model does not constitute an outright rejection of competition, nor of a striving for excellence; but critically it does, as Fairchild (1994) has it: 'reject the ... exclusionary emphasis on winning in which all those who do not win are understood as losers.'

---

[2] I am indebted to Fairchild (1994) for this account of Nelson's models of sport.

A *delicate balancing act*

A consideration of sport as social practice and social institution emphasizes the inherent and inescapable tension between the realization of internal and external goods. To understand this duality of sport, it is useful to think of sport as two sides of the same coin, in so far as sport has two **inseparable** dimensions. One side or dimension denotes the constitutive features of the social *practice* of sport – a collaborative project which displays features of association, cooperation and competition. The other side of the coin is turned towards the contextual features of the *institution* of sport. As a widespread social practice, sports attract the interest and influence of other social institutions and it is easy to see how educational, commercial and political organizations promote their specific interests beyond or external to those provided by the internal goods of sport as a social practice.

A list of current social problems, issues and changes in sports practice would include:

- performance-enhancing substance abuse
- performer violence, cheating, gamesmanship
- incidence of deviant behaviour by coaches
- abuse and exploitation of athletes
- illegal inducements for performers and promoters
- rule and format changes to accommodate the demands of television and sponsors.

Most of these and other social problems and issues arise when the social practices of sport and their internal goods are compromised by external imperatives. Chapter 2 considers the current developments in sport which give rise to these external pressures and thereby threaten the integrity of sports practices.

chapter two

Sports: change and development

Characteristics of modern sports

Modern sport forms are a product of the industrial era, the characteristic features of which are identified by Guttmann (1978). He provides a broad historical sweep of games and sports from ancient to modern times to argue that modern sports differ from pre-industrial games, sports, recreations and rituals in several respects. The difference lies in the fact that modern sports exhibit seven interrelated characteristics which have never before appeared together. These are:

- secularism
- equality
- specialization
- rationalization
- bureaucratization
- quantification
- records.

Secularism
In this context, secularism refers to the observation that modern sports are not directly linked to religious beliefs, worship or rituals as they have been in the past. As Guttmann (1978) puts it:

> Modern sports are not intended to transcend the material world; instead they embody the immediacy and values of the material world.

Of course, many people, both participants and spectators, care passionately about sports – which occupy much of their emotional, intellectual and physical energies. From different theoretical perspectives, Elias and Dunning (1986) and Hoffman (1992) argue that modern sports are, in a secular society, of quasi-religious significance, but this is precisely because sports are no longer part of the sacred world.

Equality

Sporting challenges are a communistic, egalitarian Utopia where everyone, regardless of their social, national or ethnic background, is faced with the same set of competitive conditions and, as Caillois (1961) notes, an equality of chance. This is assured by the constitutive rules which contain an assumption that the search for equality should guide the playing of modern sports. As Metheny (1976) has it, in sport 'stripped of all excuses, man stands naked before his gods'. Of course, perfect equality never exists since there is a considerable difference in the technical, financial and professional resources which athletes can draw upon. For example, in the more technical athletic field events, athletes from the developed world have an advantage over athletes from developing countries for these reasons.

Specialization

This refers to sports performers dedicating themselves to one event or one sport, and to one position or role within a sport. Positions are defined in terms of different skills and responsibilities, an obvious example being the various codes of football. American football even allows for changing whole teams of players for attacking and defending roles. Also, specialized equipment is developed to meet the demands of both specific sports and specific roles.

Rationalization

Guttmann (1978) discusses this feature in terms of the complex of codified rules and strategies. The rules specify both the goals and the manner through which these might be achieved. For example, Rule One of the game of Basketball states:

> Basketball is played by two teams of five players each. The purpose of each team is to throw the ball into the opponents' basket and to prevent the other team from securing the ball and scoring. The ball may be passed, thrown, tapped, rolled, or dribbled in any direction, subject to the restrictions laid down in the following rules.

The other eight rules describe the ways in which this overarching aim (above) can legitimately be achieved – the complexity of which is demonstrated by the 93 'articles' needed to clarify and interpret the meaning and intention of the rules!

Therefore, the processes and the outcomes of sports are interdependent. For example, winning a game of soccer by two goals to one (the outcome) is only meaningful through the processes or means by which this outcome is achieved. Conversely, the playing processes of sports get their meanings from attempts to achieve the desired outcome.

Another connotation of rationalization, not recognized by Guttmann, is the ceaseless search for the most efficient and effective ways of winning sports contests – a connotation which leads many writers to note the ways in which much modern sports practices are adopting work-like characteristics.

Bureaucratization

As with multi-national companies, modern sports are administered and controlled by large and complex organizations from local, through regional and national, to international levels. As Guttmann observes, the people in these organizations have power to 'oversee and sanction athletes, teams, and events ... make up rules and enforce them, organise events and certify records'. As sports have diffused to different social and national groups, so the bureaucracy needed to oversee the governance of the sport has become more complex and more powerful.

Quantification
Modern sports are steeped in measurements and statistics – about times, distances, weights, scores, personal bests, league position, goals/points average, etc. These provide the basis for identifying relative achievements from individual athletes to national teams. Achievement then is expressed in measurable terms. Whitson (1986) points out that this quantitative assessment of merit is not an inherent characteristic of sport, and that qualitative judgements about the experiences in the activity could be the criteria of success.

Records
The motto of the Olympic Games is 'Citius, Altius, Fortius' – Faster, Higher, Stronger – a celebration of humankind's striving towards ever greater levels of achievement (in measurable terms!). A corollary to quantification, therefore, is an emphasis on records – from school and age records, through leagues, communities, regions, countries, continents to world records – and it is through these records (and the recording of them) that specific performances or events get their significance relative to other performances separated in space and time.

Useful as the preceding text is as a basis for considering changes in sport, Guttmann's account might be criticized on two counts. First, he provides a description but no explanation of why modern sport has the seven characteristics listed above, an explanation which can only be given through examining the nature and dynamics of modern industrial society. Secondly, although the account provides insights into differences in sporting expression **between** historical eras, little emphasis is given to the changes and developments **within** a historical (e.g. the modern) era which give rise to the social problems and issues in contemporary sport. It is to this which we now turn.

Understanding contemporary problems and issues in sports requires a sense of history, namely that the present is the product of the past, that the nature and characteristics of modern sports are related to broader social changes, and that sporting practice in the future will be influenced by the decisions and purposes of sports personnel in the present. The following does not provide a history of sports – this can be found elsewhere (Guttmann, 1978; Dunning and Sheard, 1979; Brailsford, 1988, 1992; Mason, 1988 and Cashmore, 1991). Rather, the aim will be to identify the characteristic developments, at the level of both practices and institutions, which have given rise to the social problems and issues which confront contemporary sports. Subsequent chapters will examine these developments in more detail.

Drawing upon Guttmann's account of the features of modern sports, **change** will be examined at two interdependent levels covering larger scale macro changes to the social context of sport, and smaller scale micro changes to the forms and practices of individual sports. These are interdependent in so far as changes at one level are interconnected with changes at the other. The two levels to be examined are:

- changes to **sports processes** – the structures and practices of sport
- changes to **sports worlds** – the organizational context of sports practice.

Changes to sports processes

This refers to actual instances of playing or partici-pating in sports; realizing the 'virtual' structure of a sport (as given by the codified rules) in actual practice. These sports processes, of course, range from relatively informal recreational settings to more serious, intense, elite sporting events. However, the direction of change over time is towards:

- an increasing instrumentalization
- a more intensive search for efficiency in achieving goals
- more work-like or professionalized attitudes towards the practice of sport
- an increase in the level of performance required for success (LPS)
- increased incidence of changes to the rules or formal structures of sports.

The consequences of these changes will be considered in later chapters, but for the moment it is important to note how these changes are interrelated. **Instrumentalization** refers to the trend of valuing the outcomes of sports at the expense of intrinsic dimensions which emanate from the sporting challenge – the patterns of action and experiences the sport provides, mastery, enjoyment, or the experience of 'flow' as characterized by Csikszentmihalyi (see Chapter 1). Debates about the educational aims of sport in the National Curriculum, and of sports for personal and social education in the Youth Service, (Stead and Swain, 1990) articulate around the attempt to manage the tension between intrinsic and instrumental values of sports participation which have been discussed by Snyder and Spreitzer (1978), McIntosh (1979) and Scott (1981).

Instrumentalism leads to a constant search for **increased efficiency** in achieving goals. In an industrial context, the search for efficiency results in a reformation of the production process in order to eliminate waste in terms of labour, materials and time. In one respect, sport inverts this economic formula since it cannot **rationalize** its labour force;

for example, the rules of soccer dictate the number of players per side, and the means which are sanctioned with respect to the aims of scoring and winning. However, the 'production' of modern sports requires the development of skills, tactics and strategies which become the basis of training and the means through which players compete effectively. The development of notational and other video analyses in sports contexts is a contemporary example of how players and coaches seek to rationalize the use of resources.

Some writers therefore (e.g. Brohm, 1978; Rigauer, 1982; Beamish, 1982; Eichberg, 1984) indicate how this rationalization of sport mirrors the principles of scientific management in industry – a structural similarity between sport and work.

For many participants, the experience of sport assumes **work-like** characteristics for which a **professionalization** of attitudes is both necessary and appropriate, with a consequent loss of autonomy or self-advocacy for the individual. Increasingly, sport requires more intensive preparation, prescribed diets, delayed gratification, the sublimation of other interests for the sake of sport, more structured training and playing environments, and where qualities such as self-discipline, self-belief, ambition and clear, unambiguous goals are expected; in short, an ascetic regimen of mind and body to meet the sporting challenge.

An adoption of this style of participation is demanded, since the **level of performance required for success** (LPS) increases year on year. The obsession with records (quantitatively measured), coupled with the increasingly intensive and extensive competitive schedules of most sports, impels this LPS. Increasingly, the sports competitor requires the service of supportive technical and paramedical personnel to compete effectively.

As players and coaches devise ever more efficient, more instrumentalized, more professionalized practice, so the **structures** of sport processes as provided by the **rules** are put under strain. In most team games, such as the codes of football for example, rule changes have accelerated in the postwar years. Rules committees of the governing bodies of sport, charged with maintaining and preserving the viability of the sport, have to accommodate the technical, physical, technological and strategic advances. The outcome is that the rules of sports change over time. Televisual media enable us to compare footage from sports of bygone eras with contemporary examples.

Many commentators (e.g. Elias and Dunning, 1986; Goldlust, 1987; Maguire, 1991) suggest that most rule changes (e.g. the back pass rule in soccer, fielding restrictions in one-day cricket, the tennis tie-break, changes to the ruck and maul rules in rugby union) are due to governing bodies bowing to the wishes of commerce in trying to make the sport more spectacular, better television. The impact of com-modification processes on the format, rules and scheduling of sports will be assessed in Chapter 3.

However, many rule changes are the outcome of rule-makers having to cope with players and coaches, operating in highly competitive environments, devising strategies of play which escape the inten-tions of the rule-makers (Kew, 1987, 1990). The upshot is that rules are reviewed, modified, clarified, rescinded – sometimes annually – and referees and umpires (themselves under increasing pressure to perform well) are instructed how the rules are to be enforced. Rule changes, therefore, are yet one more indication of the increasing instrumentalization and rationalization of sports processes.

Changes to sport worlds

'Sports Worlds' is not a term in common currency. Borrowing from Becker's (1984) account of 'art worlds', the term denotes the network of people who have a function in 'producing' sports processes. This includes not only the performers (the direct producers of sport processes), but also managers, trainers, coaches, scouts, officials, referees, umpires, sports psychologists, physiotherapists and sport scientists involved with specific sports (the indirect producers of sports processes). A sports world also encompasses a sport's governing body – the formal organization with its executive and committee structure, at local, regional and international levels – which administers, manages and controls each sport. Each of these separate groups of people is constituted *by virtue* of their specific functions in 'producing' sports practices either in advising the players to produce successful performances (e.g. coaches, managers), or in controlling and administering the sport (e.g. referees, governing bodies). This excludes a consideration of media and commercial influence at this juncture, since these interest groups are **not** constituted by virtue of their function in producing sport.

The above description of functional groups applies to most contemporary sports, but the main historical changes to the nature of sports worlds might be identified as follows:

- from simple to complex networks of people
- from ad hoc and amateur associations to bureaucratic and increasingly professionalized international organizations
- from traditional voluntarism to an increasing financial dependency upon both public and private capital.

From simple to complex networks

Borrowing from Bishop and Hoggett's (1986) analysis of voluntary organizations, the establishment of sporting 'associations' in the mid to late nineteenth century (e.g. soccer in 1863, rugby union in 1871) might be characterized as 'organizing around enthusiasms'. The original power of the middle and upper class governing bodies extended little further than formulating the rules of play, and even then local variations were allowed (e.g. in the powerful Sheffield League in soccer). Even the role of referee was resisted for a time, since it was assumed that any rule transgressions were unintended, and disputes could be resolved by the opposing captains.

These simple communities of interest have developed into much more complex bureaucratic networks, as these sports have been disseminated to other social groups and cultures. Increasing complexity is evident in the division of functions and delegated power to oversee the disparate elements of the organizations' work; multi-layered organizations which inevitably exhibit tensions and power struggles between the different interest groups (e.g. players and administrators).

From amateurism to professionalism

The ideology of amateurism, from the Latin 'to love', was the dominant social definition of sports when they were established in the nineteenth century. As Dunning and Sheard (1979) have it:

> Sports had as their ideal aim the production of pleasure ...
> an immediate emotional state rather than some ulterior
> end, whether of a material or other kind.

Training too hard, prizing victory too much, was anathema to true 'gentlemanly' sport enthusiasts. Professionals or subsidized players (i.e. compensated for lost wages) were often discriminated against in order to protect the social exclusiveness of sports. Some sports (e.g. cricket) reached an accommodation which allowed both professionals (gentlemen) and amateurs (players) to play alongside one another, although social distinctions were maintained, and professionals (the lower order) attained no positions of power within the organization. Indeed, right up to the dissolution of the gentlemen/players distinction in the 1960s, 'players' were primarily employed as bowlers at the gentlemen batters! Others (e.g. soccer, boxing) developed two parallel organizations, one professional, the other amateur. Tennis, athletics and Rugby Union resisted full-blown professionalism until 1968, 1988 and 1995, respectively, before finally acknowledging that amateurism was anachronistic, unsustainable, and that its defence would lead to a break up of the sport (as had happened to rugby in 1895 with the formation of the professional Northern Rugby Union, later the Rugby League). Even in fell-running (a minor regional sport in northern Britain), a ludicrous situation arose in the 1980s when members of the (professional) British Open Fell-runners Association were banned from running in events organized by the Fell-Runners Association, an amateur body affiliated to the Amateur Athletic Association!

Nowadays, the term 'amateur' has different connotations. As Cashmore (1991) notes, it has almost become a pejorative word meaning lack of refinement, unskilful, and frankly ... amateurish – in contrast to the earlier 'elevated symbol of all that was good in sport', promulgated by elite dominant groups.

Professionalism is clearly part of the new social definition of sport, but is not to be narrowly defined as payment for playing, nor to the attitudes and values of players. As sport processes have become more serious, more instrumentalized and more rationalized, so technical and scientific services (exercise physiologists, physiotherapists, biomechanicians, psychologists) have been developed with accredited qualifications, and organized into professional bodies with the requisite charters and codes of conduct as befits any profession. Moreover, extensive training courses for officials (referees, umpires, scorers and judges) have led to a graded hierarchy of levels of competence and identifiable sporting careers outside playing. Similarly, coach education programmes (run in Britain by national governing bodies and by the National Coaching Foundation which was established in 1983), accredit competence from basic 'leaders' certificates of competence to elite levels.

In some sports, formal associations of players, coaches and referees have developed, to promote their particular interests and concerns. **Sports worlds**, therefore, encompass increasingly professionalized interest groups who sell their skills and fulfil highly specific functions in producing sports, whether directly (as players) or indirectly (as all other groups).

National governing bodies have not been immune to these radical changes. Typically, they have been peopled by volunteers who served the interests of members and, by their own constitutions, are non-profit-making. Yet they are now being required by the Sports Council, as a condition of funding, to produce development plans, set strategic objectives and generally to adopt business practices in their organization and everyday practices. Abrams and Wolsey (1996) indicate the difficulties associated with these changes. Over the decades, sports organizations have developed sedimented practices and, as they put it, **distinctive cultures** which inevitably are resistant to change, making it 'difficult to adjust to the increased need to become more professional and business-like in their operations'.

From voluntarism to financial dependency

In 1972, the Sports Council gained executive status. This, for the first time in Britain, enabled government to provide grant aid to national governing bodies and other sports organizations to promote the twin strategies of mass participation and the creation of excellence in sport. Prior to this date, sports had typically relied upon the fees of members, some small-scale local sponsors, and fund-raising efforts by members of the relevant organization. Sports, traditionally being associated with play and voluntary activities, had not, other than the funding of school sport through the Recreation and Physical Fitness Act 1937, been seen as an aspect of social welfare. However, since the 1970s, governing bodies for sport have been recommended (if not required) by the state to provide equitable opportunity for disadvantaged groups in society, such as the disabled, ethnic minorities and unemployed people. Grant aid is available for such initiatives, as well as for capital projects, especially through the National Lottery.

Beyond the state sector, the most significant development is the increasing financial dependency of sport on the commercial sector. Hargreaves (1986) argues that the 'sponsorship–advertising–media axis' is the key factor in the present redevelopment of sport (see Chapter 3). Sports organizations and (some) participants receive revenue from television coverage, from advertising and from sponsorship of events, clothing, leagues and cups. This influence is not benign and gives rise to an asymmetrical relationship within which the interests of commerce begin to outweigh the interests of sports. Hargreaves writes:

> Dependency is such that sport cannot afford to ignore the wishes of advertisers and sponsors ... indeed they must learn to anticipate their wishes ... corporate capital uses sport increasingly as an adjunct to capital accumulation, and in so doing pulls sport more into its orbit.

As an example of how this is manifest in practice, Figure 2.1 draws together all three of these indices of change in sports worlds with respect to one sport, namely the development of basketball in Britain over a twenty-year period.

Different sports, different problems

The changes identified above are generally applicable to influences which have shaped or conditioned all

1970	1990
ABBA	*EBBA*
Structure	
National Executive committee (10 members)	National Executive committee (16 members)
No full-time professional officers	6 full-time professional officers (secretary, senior technical, competitions, regional development, marketing and development) plus 8 administrative staff
Committees	
a) International	a) International
b) Finance and General Purposes	b) Policy and Resources
c) Coaching and Officiating	c) Coaching
	d) Competitions
	e) Development
	f) Disciplinary/Appeals
	g) Officiating
	h) League Liaison
	* Ad hoc sub-committees, e.g. drugs.
Technical Qualifications	
a) Coaching grades: Grades 1 and 2	a) Coaching: 5 (Senior/1/2/Prelim/Leader)
b) Refereeing grades: Grades 1 and 2	b) Refereeing: 5 (1/2/3/Prelim/Junior)
	c) Table Officials: Grades 1 and 2
Competitions	
a) Regional competitions: men	a) British Basketball League (1986)
b) National Knock-out Cup: men	b) National Basketball League
	c) Division 1 (men/women) (1972)
	Division 2 (men) (1988)
	Division 2 (women) (1988)
	NBL Regionalized Division 3 (men/women) (1989)
	d) National Knock-out Cups (men/women/juniors)
	e) Junior Men's Regional League
Specialist Organizations	
a) English Schools Basketball Association (1957)	a) ESBA
	b) English Mini BB Association

	c) GB Wheelchair BB Association
	d) GB Wheelchair Officials Association
	e) English Association of Basketball Officials (EABO) 1981
	f) Basketball Coaches Association of England (BCAE) (1978)
	g) Players Association

Sponsorship	
None	a) Carlsberg UK
	b) National Westminster Bank (British Basketball League)
	c) Coca Cola GB
	d) Converse UK Ltd
	e) Spalding Sports Ltd
	f) Mitre Sports
	g) American Airlines

NB. Similar structures to the EBBA have been developed in all four home countries; whereas in 1970 the ABBA organized basketball in England, Scotland, Wales and northern Ireland.

Figure 2.1 Basketball 1970–90: from simple to complex sport-world

contemporary sport, but not all sports are subject to these changes in the same way, at the same rate or at the same time. There are currently over 120 national governing bodies of sport in Britain and many others worldwide. Some of these administer activities which can only in an extended sense be called 'sports' (e.g. aerobics, marbles, skittles), but it is useful to distinguish between sports which are relatively 'central' and those which are relatively 'marginal' in British sporting culture. The indices of centrality/ marginality, although not all present in every case, include the:

● extent of their practice as evidenced by data about participation rates

- distribution of their practice among identifiable social groups according to age, gender, ethnicity, and social class
- extent of commercial penetration by commerce, sponsors, advertisers
- extent of televisual and print media coverage
- level of funding by the state.

Marginal sports tend to have fewer participants, from more homogeneous social groups, and have greater difficulty in attracting commercial sponsorship and media coverage. Typically, these would include most women's sports (especially those which do not conform to dominant images of femininity), age-group sports (both younger and older participants), sports for disabled people, and so-called 'minor' sports such as lacrosse, fell-running, orienteering, fencing. Sporting activity such as these cannot support professionalism, are reliant on state and/or voluntary funding for their development, and participants, even at the higher levels, have to meet the costs of their own involvement. Contrast, for example, the earning power of England's current male Rugby Union squad with their female counterparts (the World Cup winners), who can get no sponsorship, whose only income comes from subscriptions and gate money and who even have to buy their own kit! Contrast also the experience of Oxford University rowers as depicted in the following article by Cleary (1995):

> The men have spent the last six months surrounded by gadgets, gurus, gymnasiums and a sackful of sponsor's loot with which to fund their high-tec, high profile strategy.... Beefeater Gin are giving £1.5 million over three years to the men. The Oxford women have two sponsors: March Communications in Kingston who gave them £1000, and 'Fasta Pasta' in Oxford, who have fed them for the last few weeks. Even the committed can tire of tagliatelle night, noon, and morning.

Any analysis of critical developments in modern sports must be sensitive to variations across different types and levels of its practice. Different sports have different problems in managing change and planning for their future.

A critical note

The main thrust of the analysis in this section has been to note developmental trends that threaten to undermine the integrity of sports practices. A more radical perspective is developed by Gruneau (1983) and Eichberg (1984), both of whom are interested in fostering and celebrating physical activities alternative to modern sport, primarily because they suggest that modern sport is beyond redemption. Eichberg, for example, cites four forms of bodily exercise which are free of the excesses of modern sports. These are (a) indigenous and national games, (b) expressive activities, (c) meditative activities, and (d) outdoor activities. Each of these, unsullied by national or global commercial imperatives, are social spaces which provide a qualitatively different experience of involvement, which do not brutalize individuals, and which allow a degree of individual control over the activity. Some radical feminists develop similar arguments (see Chapter 7). This radicalism is not to be taken lightly, for it underscores the necessity for sports to address these issues seriously!

Chapter 1 located the source of contemporary debates about social problems as an irreducible tension between sport as social practice and social institution. This chapter has addressed the long-term changes to sports which typically give rise to current social problems and issues. These are the focus of the rest of Part One.

Sports in the marketplace

Introduction

> Sports have allied themselves so irrevocably to television that they have lost the ability to control their own destiny (Hart, 1976).

This was written two decades ago, before the full-scale influence of commerce on sport had been realized, but strikes at the heart of a critical issue for sport – the relative powerlessness of sports organizations to resist the blandishments of commerce. A process of accommodation has meant that, for many sports, the bulk of their income comes from non-sporting business interests. The same applies to professional sportspeople who earn more by marketing themselves and endorsing products than from actual sports performances.

Since their establishment in the nineteenth century, there has been money in sport, and entrepreneurs in sports such as boxing, soccer and motor sports, have sought to make financial capital out of their practice. Nevertheless, arguably the most far-reaching and powerful influence on contemporary sports is a highly developed process of '*commodification*' (sometimes called commoditization). This refers to the ways in which sports are being increasingly shaped by a market rationality. Sports are not just played, coached and administered, but are also packaged and 're-presented' as spectacles to be sold to consumers for a profit. Even non-profit sports organizations are being required to reorganize themselves along business lines.

Some would regard this commercial involvement as a benign and beneficial influence, providing much needed finance to enable sports organizations to promote and develop their sports – a symbiotic relationship where both commerce and sports benefit. This is certainly the position taken by the Sports Council in Britain, in line with current government policy to cut back on public spending, and to encourage sports organizations to seek private sector funding.

Others take a more critical perspective to indicate the exploitative nature of the sport/capital relationship, since it is the profit-making interests of capital which override the interests of sport – an asymmetrical power relationship which can lead to a prostituting of sport before the altar of commerce, leading ultimately to a denial of sport. The key issue, therefore, is how to manage the process in order to protect the integrity of sport in the face of potentially exploitative and manipulative commercial interests.

Sport and capital

Most people's image of commercial interest in sport is confined to the sponsorship of high-profile events like the Olympics, or domestic competitions such as soccer's Premier League. But sports relationship to capital is far more complex. Hargreaves (1986) identifies four ways in which capital is related to sport:

1 As a profit-maximizing business enterprise in which investment functions to accumulate capital, and where capitalists own, control or organize the business. Hargreaves cites professional boxing, motor sports and horse-racing as examples. In professional boxing, for example, the fracturing of its international organization into four associations leads to a plethora of 'world champions', while powerful managers and agents act as commodity brokers, the commodity being the fighters. In the leisure sector, the private develop-

ment of health and fitness centres, squash clubs, ice-skating and ten-pin bowling arenas are also profit-maximizing enterprises.

2 Sports which seek not to maximize profit for private capital, but to operate at least at cost in order to remain viable. Most voluntary associations operate according to this logic, whereby surplus income is used to develop facilities, improve the administrative and coaching infrastructure of the sport, or to fund youth and other development programmes.

However, National Governing Bodies are now required to produce development plans and set strategic objectives. These external demands mean that increasingly they have to become more professional and businesslike in their operations; an imperative which gives rise to tensions and conflicts as voluntary associations are being asked to change their sedimented culture and practice (Abrams and Wolsey, 1996).

3 As a widespread social practice, sport can stimulate the accumulation of capital indirectly by providing a market for goods and services associated with it. This includes specialist clothing and sports equipment, the design and building of facilities and the gambling industry (e.g. the Football Pools, the Tote).

4 Sport functions as a sales adjunct to aid capital accumulation by the non-sporting commercial sector. This is achieved through the medium of sponsorship (of events, competitions, development programmes, clubs, individual athletes), and advertising at events, in published material, and most importantly, on television.

Taken together, these four sets of relationships represent a multi-million pound industry, incorporating both participation and consumption of sports, and from elite to grass-roots levels. The Sports Council estimated that, in 1992, £9.75 billion was

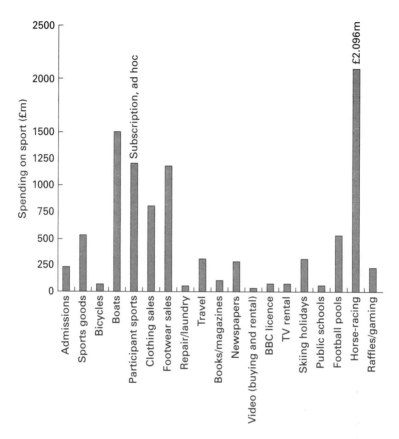

Figure 3.1 Spending on sport in Britain – financial winners, 1992
(*Source*: Sports Council, as reported in 'The Guardian', 22 June 1993, p. 10, by permission of 'The Guardian' newspaper)

spent on sport and sports-related goods in Britain – more than double the amount for 1986. Figure 3.1 shows how the money was spent.

Sport as a sales adjunct to make money for the non-sporting commercial sector is the dimension which arguably has had the most impact on the nature and structures of sports and on the governance of their practice. This provides the main focus of this chapter.

Sponsorship

Sponsorship means financial and/or material support for activities existing independently of the sponsor's primary commercial concern, yet from which the sponsor might reasonably hope to gain commercial benefit. Expenditure on sports sponsorship in the UK was £210 million in 1989, £256 million in 1994, and is expected to rise to £286 million by 1998. According to Mintel Leisure Intelligence, sport accounts for 56% of the total sponsorship market, with the arts on 15% and social/environmental organizations on 4%. Sponsorship is neither spread evenly among sports nor within sports. The main market is firmly with *male* professional sports, and with the key events associated with these sports. With an eye on the male consumer and the manly image of sport, coupled with the low visibility of women's sport through poor television coverage, sponsors largely shun women's sport (Birkett,1993).

In terms of capital investment, the principal sponsoring industries in UK sport are tobacco (denied through legislation from direct product promotion on TV), oil, alcoholic drinks, financial institutions, tyre manufacturers, food and confectionery, sports equipment manufacturers, clothing manufacturers and bookmakers. Table 3.1 illustrates the size of this market by listing the current main sponsors of four sports in Britain.

According to 'The Guardian' newspaper (22 June 1993), a sponsor's name on a football shirt appearing in every Sunday newspaper is estimated to be worth about £100,000 in free publicity. Hence one can understand why Carlsberg were willing to pay £1 million to Liverpool FC to have their name emblazoned on home and away strips for one season. Most recently, professional soccer has become the target of computing and 'high tech' business (e.g. AST's sponsorship of Aston Villa), replacing the traditional association of soccer with beer and lager. For most

Table 3.1 Principal sponsors of four sports in Britain

Athletics	Motor-racing	Cricket	Football
Mobil	Marlboro	Cornhill Insurance	Coca-cola
Lucozade	John Player	Benson & Hedges	Sharp
Mars	Shell	NatWest	JVC
Pearl Assurance	Castrol	John Player	GM Vauxhall
Kodak	Texaco	Castlemaine XXXX	Barclays Bank
TSB	Benetton	Tetley Bitter	Carling Black Label
Seiko	Camel	Prudential Assurance	NEC
McDonalds	Benson & Hedges	Britannic Assurance	Canon
Nutrasweet	Canon	AXA Equity & Law	Beazer Homes
	Labatts	Texaco	B & Q
			Endsleigh

Source: by permission BMRB Mintel.

professional soccer clubs, sponsorship income is greater than gate money, while for many top class professional sportspersons, money from sponsorship and product endorsement far outweighs prize money earned.

Events, clubs, tournaments, leagues and individual players are all commodities to be marketed and to attract the sponsor's interest in advertising commercial products. One of the most successful agencies to manage this process is currently Mark McCormack's International Management Group (IMG), specialists in sports marketing, consultancy and programme planning. Clients include the English Football Association, the British Open Golf Championship, Wimbledon and even – when he visited Britain in 1982 – the Pope! IMG takes an average 10% of all prize-money, and 25% of a player's earnings from merchandizing and endorsement deals. One of IMG's most recent recruits is the British tennis player Tim Henman, whose much-publicized success at Wimbledon 1996 brought an avalanche of sponsorship deals. His marketability is expected to earn him £1 million from a tennis racket manufacturer, £1 million from Adidas for wearing their sportswear, £250,000 from media work and a similar sum from personal appearances.

Contrast this, however, with the plight of many elite British athletes in low-profile sports, where even Olympic representation does not ensure financial security. A survey conducted by the British Olympic Association after the Barcelona Olympics in 1992 found that only 38% received sponsorship and, of these, only 5% got more than £10,000 a year. Only 23% had ever won any prize money, of whom 62% had a lifetime total of less than £1000. Most elite athletes in Britain depend upon grants from the Sports Aid Foundation which in 1995 handed out just over £2 million to approximately 3000 individuals from more than 50 sports. These grants are not large. For an international competitor just outside the world's top six, grant-aid is limited to between £2000 and £4000 per year. Compared with other developed countries, the level of state support for elite sports competitors in Britain is derisory, and the relatively poor results at the Atlanta Olympics confirms the financial investment necessary for international sporting achievement. For many, international success is achieved despite of, rather than because of, support from public or private sources.

In the present context, the critical point to note is the limitations of a market-driven approach to funding elite sports performers. Super-elite sportspersons, in high-profile sports such as athletics and tennis, are highly marketable, but the large majority, in sports such as archery and judo, have to rely on private family resources, unemployment benefit, and/or small state grants. Amateurism, at least in terms of public funding for elite sports, is not dead in Britain.

Sponsorship of professional sports stood up well to the effects of the recession in the early 1990s – an indication of the surplus value that sports sponsorship has for business. At the other end of the market, where a degree of social altruism is evident, local sponsorship declined during the recession. Sportsmatch was launched by government in 1992 to raise funds for local sport. Under this scheme, administered in England by the Institute of Sports Sponsorship, government pledges to match every £1 raised by business sponsors for local sports. Nevertheless, there is a massive difference in the interest of business in elite and grass-roots sport. A recent survey by Systems 3 business analysts identified several reasons why commercial enterprises want to sponsor sport. These included improving public relations, enhancing the company image, specific brand promotion, press and television coverage, an opportunity to entertain clients through corporate hospitality schemes, improving staff relations, and an opportunity for social altruism. Overall, however, the direct return for sponsoring companies will not be in sales, but rather in brand and corporate awareness. The sponsorship consultancy APA, in 1995, emphasized the importance of good matchmaking between the sport and the commercial product.

> The fit is between understanding what motivates your target audience and looking at areas where you can become commercially involved. It is also important to understand the imagery and associations you get reflected from the sport or event.

The attraction of sport for business sponsors can only be fully appreciated, however, by considering sponsorship in conjunction with the televisual media.

The sponsorship–advertising–media axis

The term 'sponsorship–advertising–media axis', coined by Hargreaves (1986), stresses the interdependence of commercial interests in sport. These interdependent interests are key factors in the present redevelopment of sport, and provide a basis for taking a more critical perspective on the impact of commerce on sport and issues about the integrity of sports which result. Some, however, would argue that the interests of sponsors, advertisers and the media in sport is a match made in heaven, where everyone benefits. Players have gained financially through appearance money, player contracts and endorsements, with earnings now reflecting the true market value of their abilities. Sponsors and advertisers have benefited through specific brand promotion, through enhancing the company image among potential clients and through press and television coverage. Governing bodies gain by using corporate finance to develop and promote their sport. As one Regional Sports Council has it:

> Sports sponsorship is the only team game where both sides can win ... it is a very powerful yet cost-effective medium.

Sports administrators can also point to the promotional power of television, watched by over 90% of the British population. Gymnastics enjoyed a participation boom in the 1970s through the exploits of gymnasts such as Olga Korbut and Nadia Comenechi at successive Olympics. The profile of field hockey was raised through the British triumph at the Seoul Olympics. The relative success of recent English Rugby Union teams has enabled improvements in both youth development schemes and in facility provision.

In the last three years, Channel 4 has televised over fifty sports – not just event coverage, but information-giving programmes for potential participants. The development of cable and satellite television has increased choice for the sports fan, giving access to international events, and challenging the traditional parochialism and conservatism of BBC and ITV who continue to direct most of their sports coverage to the staple diet of snooker, soccer, horse-racing, cricket and rugby, and to the 'heritage' events such as Wimbledon, the Boat Race, the Grand National, the Derby and the Five Nations rugby championship. For the owners and controllers of the media, sport is a sure-fire winner. Between 15% and 20% of all television is devoted to sport, and it is one of the few subjects that can command a large audience outside peak-viewing times – which is why media moguls such as Rupert Murdoch and Kerry Packer (a) want to wrest control of sports from international governing bodies, and (b) want to wrest the coverage of major sports like Rugby Union and soccer, and major events such as the Olympics, from traditional terrestrial TV stations.

But do both sides win – or are there problems for the social practice of sport from the increasingly commercialized institutional context within which it is developing? Whannel (1991) calls the sport/television interdependence 'an unholy alliance', and critical perspectives about the commodification of sports contain the following arguments.

First for most people, sport means television sport – as passive consumers of images rather than actual producers of sporting events. Rather than the *actual* excitement of participating, televised sport provides a *vicarious* excitement of razzamatazz, thrills and spectacle. Jennifer Hargreaves (1987) talks of televised sport as 'a consumption opiate like sex, drugs, and drink' providing for an escape from the normal, the mundane, the ordinariness of everyday life. In an increasingly secularized society, sports events assume a quasi-religious significance, the top sportspeople become media-promoted icons for starry-eyed consumers, and sporting images and themes are remorselessly used in the selling of commodities – about which modern youth is largely uncritical. Media sport, according to this argument, encourages a passivity, a blunting of critical faculties.

Secondly, a critical perspective, as expounded by Hall (1977), stresses that the media is responsible for providing a 'selective construction of social knowledge, of the social imagery through which we perceive the world'. The media are not benign, neutral mirrors of sports practices. Rather, they contour what counts as sport, and what is important about sport, ignoring most sports practice and selectively re-presenting events which they choose to cover. A typical example of the latter is television's coverage of events such as high-profile marathons (e.g. BBC's coverage of the London Marathon and Eurosport's coverage of the Boston Marathon). These events are reconstructed as two stories: the first is the sharp end of winning and losing the elite men's and women's races, the second is about community involvement, interviewing plodders in strange costumes. What is ignored in both commentary and camera shots are the superb achievements of hundreds of serious athletes who do not fall into either of the above two categories. For example, a few years ago the winner of the women's London marathon was accompanied all the way by a 52-year-old runner from Lancashire who, in doing so, broke the world record for his age-group – the commentary was silent on this outstanding feat.

Thirdly, the media, as Hall (1977) has it, are 'socially, economically, and technically organised apparatuses for the production of messages' – messages which naturalize particular modes of perceiving sport and which, according to Sewart (1987), actually corrupts the structures and practices of sports in the interests of presenting spectacles for the armchair consumer. Sewart argues that when sport is valued as a commodity governed by a market rationality, there is little regard for sport's intrinsic content or form. He cites three ways in which the exigencies of the market have intruded into sports:

- changes to the rules, format and scheduling of sports
- the abandonment of the ethic of skill democracy
- the inclination to spectacle and theatricality.

Changes to rules, format and scheduling

Rules
If sports are to be commodities, then their actual form or structure must be consumer-friendly. Rule changes have accelerated in the last three decades paralleling the increasing dependency of sport on commerce. Changes are made to speed up the action and minimize stoppages to play, to display the quintessential skills of the sport, to stop negative defensive play which stultifies creative and exciting attacking play. The efforts of legislators are not always successful, but they are under pressure from television executives to make the sport more spectacular, and more accessible to viewers who may not have a detailed knowledge of the sport. As Elias and Dunning (1986) argue, changes to the rules or structures of sports is an outcome of tipping the balance towards the interests of spectators, and away from the interests of players. Below are a

selection of rule changes (actual or proposed) precipitated by the perceived need to spectacularize sport:

- Rugby Union – changes to the kicking laws in the 22-metre area; the differential penalty; the 5-point try; changes to the tackle, ruck and maul laws.
- Soccer – changes to the offside rule, the backpass rule; sanctions for 'professional' fouls.
- Rugby League – the 6-tackle and 'turnover' rule; the advantage laws; the offside laws at play-the-ball.
- Squash – proposals to limit the length of rallies; 15-point games; scoring on every point.
- Baseball – larger strike zone; decreasing the height of the pitcher's mound; changes to the pitching rules.
- US football – moving goalposts to back of end zone; 'sudden death' periods at tied games; changes to kick-off rule, the 2-minute rule.
- Field hockey – rescind offside rule; continuous substitutions; rescind obstruction/turning rule.
- Netball – proposals to move goalposts off back line to allow 360-degree shooting; two instead of three zones for greater freedom of movement.
- Basketball – the 30-second rule; the 3-point shot; abolition of the zone defence; changing the penalties for intentional fouls in the last three minutes of play.

Here is but one example of current thinking about rule changes in one sport to make it more spectator-friendly. O'Regan (1995), writing for aficionados of Rugby Union, argues:

> The perceived negativity of Rugby Union was the main reason behind the recent introduction of southern hemisphere-inspired law changes which soon became known as 'use it or lose it'. Australian Rugby Union has always been under commercial pressure from the more popular games of League and Aussie Rules and has been much more disposed to mould its product in order to appeal to the masses. To the

uninitiated, a rolling maul or scrum is utterly mystifying and not as thrilling as seeing someone running in open space with the ball in their hands. In the battle for larger crowds and more television coverage, there is a general feeling that Union should get the ball in play for a greater percentage of the time in order to entertain the paying public.

Format

Changes to the format of sports is even more radical, the clearest example being the advent of one-day cricket. Taking its lead from Kerry Packer's World Series Cricket in the 1970s, cricket is now played under floodlights, with multi-coloured strips, a white ball, restrictions on field placings to discourage defensive play and encourage big hitting, microphones and miniature cameras on the wickets – all this being framed and embellished by television technographics.

In golf, the relative demise of match play at the expense of stroke play competitions is media-driven. The development of climbing walls has spawned the creation of indoor climbing competitions with associated television coverage, sponsorship and advertising, and full-time highly trained professional climbers – a far cry from the purist's conception of the iconoclastic challenge of natural boulders, cliffs and mountains. At the soccer World Cup in 1994, the US media proposed a number of radical changes (e.g. widening the goals, splitting the game into four quarters, time-outs) to make the game more attractive to spectators and to allow more advertising time to be sold.

Scheduling

US television networks provide the major income of the Olympics – $401 million for Barcelona 1992 and $500 million for Atlanta 1996 – and can therefore influence the scheduling of events to catch the prime-time viewing in the USA (and hence maximize advertising revenue). The Los Angeles men's marathon, for example, was run at the hottest part of the day to accommodate the media's demands. Boxing matches are frequently scheduled in the middle of the night for similar reasons. In US Football, the scheduling of matches between the Eastern and Western Conferences has to accommodate the east/west coast time differences. The scheduling of English Premier League soccer fixtures, and the start and restart of particular matches has to accommodate similar media demands. Sky TV, having won the exclusive rights to live broadcasts of the Premier League, are in a position to demand scheduling fixtures across the whole week at peak viewing times. There have been occasions where rugby and soccer matches have gone ahead as scheduled despite appalling weather (e.g. snow, flooded pitches) because of media demands, but making a mockery of the contest. Whose interests are being served? Certainly not the players!

Abandonment of the ethic of skill democracy

This is a serious charge since it questions the very basis upon which sports are founded – one of the few areas of social life in which rational meritocratic principles apply – where the rules provide an equality of chance. One source of the abiding appeal of sports is that sometimes – just sometimes – the underdog wins against all the odds. These are events which enter into the folklore of sports. Predictable outcomes are the death-knell of sport. Yet the denial of the meritocratic principle is evident in Sewart's (1987) research into boxing and tennis. The four boxing associations, he claims, manipulate the rankings lists in the quest for 'world' title fights which will appeal to the television networks. Fighters are compelled to 'sign up' with particular managers who wield considerable influence among the WBC, WBA, IBF and WBO organizations. With respect to tennis, he suggests:

Players often 'tank' matches so that they can quit a tournament and speed off to another which offers more money; players accommodate top broadcasting demands for certainty in air time; i.e. players will split the first two sets and play an honest third to ensure filling a time slot and thus guaranteeing advertising revenue for the TV networks; players will make advance arrangements to split prize money regardless of the outcome of the match; and preferential treatment is accorded to big-name players by match umpires who are under heavy pressure from tournament directors to treat them well.

Inclination to spectacle and theatricality

The media provides a selective and active re-presentation of sport. The commercial media (a) selects between sports to choose those which make good entertainment, and (b) selects within particular sporting events to maximize spectator/viewer interest (Goldlust, 1987). Let us consider these in turn.

The media does not make an arbitrary selection, but contours what counts as 'important' events within the sporting calendar. Recently, the National Heritage Committee appealed successfully to government to ensure that key national events would continue to be broadcast on terrestrial television in the face of competition from the satellite and cable companies. BBC and ITV focus primarily upon a few sports, notably team games and horse-racing. Many sports are ignored by TV, and even in those sports which do receive coverage, the selecting process screens out most women's sport, most age-group sport, most disabled sport and most non-elite sport.

Among those sports which are televised, the events are reconstructed by giving attention to the spectacular, the dramatic, the thrills and spills, the knock-out punch, the personality clashes, the brawls on the field, the goalmouth action. A sustained entertainment is achieved by techniques including specific camera angles, slow-motion, stop motion, action replays, split screens and multiple images. These are 'high-gloss presentations' which ... 'edit events down to lean action' (Cashmore, 1991). Some sports, such as ice hockey, have developed a subculture of violence where it is expected that 'enforcers' in a team will initiate brawls and intimidate the opposition – a development which, it is suggested, is actually encouraged by media companies because it makes the action more sensational, more spectacular, and more marketable!

The epitome of this trend towards the spectacular, the dramatic, the theatrical is the development of 'made-for-TV sports' such as The World's Strongest Man, Superstars, The Survival of the Fittest, and Gladiators (which by pandering to nationalism, has recently developed an international dimension). There are also daredevil 'stunts', including alligator wrestling, clearing buses on motorbikes and cliff-diving.

Beyond these events, which at least loosely conform to conventional meritocratic principles, lies the world of buffoonery described by Sewart (1987). These are epitomized by 'knock-yourself-out' and belly-flop competitions and also include WWF events – a debauchery and trivialization of the ancient Olympic sport of wrestling. As in children's cartoons, good is pitted against evil, and 'athletes' such as Killer Kalowski and the Mongolian Stomper 'compete' in 'matches' entitled Texas Bull-rope, Steel Cage, or Indian Death. Sewart calls these 'trash sports' – a denial of the axiomatic principles which are the basis for sport – and he recognizes the overwhelming power of television in the shift towards a market rationality thus:

> Instead of sports contests which happen to be broadcast on television, the process of commodification has given us television events which happen to involve sports.

Other critical perspectives include Clarke and Clarke's (1982) assessment that the values of spectacle, drama, personalization and immediacy inform the presentation of sport by the televisual media.

Similarly, Duncan and Brummett (1987) discuss the 'media logic' of TV's representation of spectator sport, the four characteristics of which are:

- narrative (TV sport is mediated as a 'story' with 'characters', and with endemic conflict)
- intimacy (TV sport focuses on individuals, on personalities, on emotions, on creating a one-to-one relationship between viewer and player)
- commodification (TV sports advertising fused with the content of sports, players are packaged and merchandised)
- time segments (TV sport coverage blocked into rigid, short (5–10 second), intense scenes, sport packaged to fit advertising slots).

The selectivity of the media is not confined to television. In an analysis of the sports magazine 'Sports Illustrated', Davis (1993) argues that the magazine (a) beckons consumers who are white, western, affluent, heterosexual, men; (b) marginalizes women's sports, thereby reinforcing an image of sport as a male preserve, and (c) is influenced by advertisers who show a lack of interest in reaching those who cannot afford to buy their products.

At root, all the issues around media sport are about power – in this case the relative power between media and sports organizations. Gurevitch (1991) argues that in an era of global communication, the power of the media has been enhanced; television cannot be regarded as a passive observer, but rather has become an integral part of, and actively constructs, the reality it chooses to cover. Nowhere is this more true than in the case of media-sports!

Globalization

As Critcher (1979) points out, sport has been influenced by complex processes of modernization:

internationalized, professionalized, commercialized, spectacularized and, most recently, globalized. The increased intensity of commodifying sports practices does not happen in isolation, but rather is part of much broader global processes. Jarvie and Maguire (1994) argue that all of our lives are intimately connected with unfolding **globalization** processes.

These processes include the emergence of a global economy, a transnational cosmopolitan culture and a range of international social movements. A multitude of transnational or global economic and technological exchanges, communication networks and migratory patterns characterizes this interconnected world pattern.

Media-sport is part of this pattern of interdependence and becomes a 'global cultural product' produced by transnational corporations and transmitted to consumers all over the world. Drawing upon the work of Appadurai (1990), Jarvie and Maguire discuss five interconnected dimensions or 'scapes' to this globalization process :

(a) **ethnoscapes**: the international movement of people
(b) **technoscapes**: the flow of machinery and plant produced by business corporations and governments
(c) **financescapes**: the flow of money/capital around the globe
(d) **mediascapes**: the flow of images and information by print and audio-visual media
(e) **ideoscapes**: the flow of ideas and ideologies associated with states or social movements.

Each of these is evident in the production and consumption of sport in the world market, some examples of which are provided below.

1 Ethnoscapes: sports tourists; migrant sports workers (players, managers, coaches), e.g. US

basketball players in the UK, in Canada, foreign soccer players in the Premier League, British coaches abroad; 'exiles' with dual nationality such as Zola Budd.

2 Technoscapes: the design, manufacture and financing of sports equipment (e.g. Mitre, Nike, Reebok) in different parts of the world; the building of sports facilities by transnational companies; international drug-testing.

3 Financescapes: the international trade in appearance money, prize money, (e.g. marathons), endorsements of commercial products; world circuits (e.g. tennis, golf); Grand Prix events (e.g. athletics, motor sports); the marketing of American sports (e.g. American football, basketball).

4 Mediascapes: the growth of satellite and cable technology; new market segmentation; made-for-TV sports events; increase in the number of top level competitions (e.g. Grand Prix circuits); a shift from shared national sporting rituals to a fragmented international audience (Williams, 1995).

5 Ideoscapes: transnational celebrations of sport and culture such as the Olympics, the soccer World Cup; increased knowledge of other cultures, of alternative sporting counter-cultures.

Jarvie and Maguire, Gurevitch, and Williams, all stress that the outcome of these globalization processes is not a homogenization of culture, but rather they help to legitimate and reposition counter-cultures and other stirrings against the existing social order.

Some key questions

The critical problems and issues arising from the commodification of sports might be summarized in the following key questions.

Where does the money go?

The impact of commerce is uneven across sports. High-profile sports in the full glare of media attention attract sponsorship, low-profile sports do not. For the latter, an issue is how to persuade anyone to sponsor them, how to attract some television exposure, if only for promotional purposes, and therefore, how to market and develop their sport successfully. For the former, an important issue is to persuade sponsors to invest in longer term developmental and promotional strategies at grass-roots level, rather than in single elite high-profile events. Also, *within* elite levels of a sport, the rewards differ markedly. Icons such as Linford Christie and Sally Gunnell can command massive salaries, but other elite performers – just below the top rank – struggle to gain any sponsorship, rely on Sports Aid Foundation grants, and have to seek other employment, or even unemployment benefit and family support, in order to sustain their involvement in sport. Financial rewards from sport diminish markedly below the very top of the pile, and differ markedly between sports.

Who rules ?

> The International Board must assert its right to govern the game rather than deliver that right to media moguls who, by definition, are more interested in their own profits than the welfare of the game.

This was written by Cain (1995) in response to the strategies adopted by the media conglomerates of Rupert Murdoch and Kerry Packer who have wanted to transform the elite levels of Rugby Union since it went 'open' in 1995. It is a murky world, where ideals and loyalty towards a particular sport collide with overwhelming monetary incentives. For example, according to Cain, the captain of the South African team has accepted a 'retainer' of £300 000 from Kerry Packer to act as an agent, essentially to persuade his fellow Springboks (the World Cup champions) to sign up for Packer's World Rugby Corporation. Individual rugby unions cannot possibly compete with this – but one example of the asymmetrical relationship between capital and sport.

Another example of shifting power is the public flotation of soccer clubs on the stock market. The income potential of soccer (through merchandizing, replica football strips, the anticipated growth of pay-per-view TV) is recognized by city traders. Of the top ten performing companies in 1996, three are sports-related; Manchester United's shares rose by 224 per cent, Leeds United's by 338 per cent and Celtic's by 488 per cent.

A final example is the power-battle ensuing from the transformation in Rugby League by the establishment of the Super League – a summer rather than winter playing season, the amalgamation of some clubs, and the exclusion of others on the basis of spectator support. In Britain, these changes are sanctioned by the governing body; in Australia, a bitter court struggle ensued between Rupert Murdoch and the Australian Rugby League reminiscent of the conflict between Kerry Packer and the International Rugby Football Union over a decade earlier.

Finally, professionalism goes beyond playing. Within sporting associations there is a shift of power away from the traditional, unpaid amateur (and more perjoratively, amateurish) administrator towards paid professionals who introduce business methods and management techniques to the running of voluntary sports associations.

Which image?

The influence of television has been portrayed in a negative light because of the selectivity of its coverage of sports, and because of its manipulation of sport in the interests of sponsors, advertisers and ultimately consumers. Sports organizations must seek ways to maximize the educational and promotional potential of TV. The growth of cable technology allows for the development of 'community' TV which might provide accessible and usable information about sporting opportunity in an immediate locality. Also, sports coverage is inherently sexist. Women's sports are comparatively neglected, receiving only 5% of all sports coverage by the entire media (Croft, 1993). This neglect means that few role models are provided for girls, and an image of female sport is perpetuated as being trivial and unimportant. When female sport is covered, there is a tendency for treatment to conform to gender stereotypes, as illustrated by Duncan's (1990) analysis of media coverage of men and women athletes at the Olympics (see Chapter 7).

Whose interests?
Elite sports performers have no control over the conditions of their practice. As noted earlier, sports performances are becoming increasingly governed by both an instrumental rationality (where successful outcomes are all-important) and by a market rationality (where the need to satisfy an audience predominates). Winning comes first, but winning with style is even better, as recent English Rugby Union teams have consistently been told by the sporting press! This lack of control relates to training regimes, strategies and styles of play adopted in performance, the scheduling of events, and the format and intensity of competitive programmes.

Whose interests – the players' or the spectators'?
To protect their interests, some sports have developed players' associations which have had some success with respect to contract rights (e.g. the Professional Footballers' Association), but their effect is relatively limited. The commercialization and instrumentalization of sports practice have arguably created an exploitative and potentially abusive environment where the rights of athletes can be overridden in the interests of capital.

Although this applies specifically to elite levels of performance, styles of play, training regimens, and coaching techniques at lower levels tend to emulate those at the higher levels, a situation which is especially critical when children are involved (Fine, 1987; Fejgin, 1994).

However, at grass-roots levels there is evidence of resistance to commercial diktats. Since going 'open', the governance of the Rugby Football Union has been contoured by the competing interests of elite clubs and players (who are best placed to exploit commercial advantages and have gone professional) and other clubs with thousands of players (who are not marketable commodities and will remain amateur). The latter, understandably, resist reorganization in the interests of the few from which they are excluded.

The commercial penetration of modern sports, particularly at elite and intensely competitive levels, creates an environment which, without careful management, encourages the corruption of sport – the focus of the following chapter.

The corruption of sports practices

Introduction

Hoberman (1992) argues that as sport has increased in social significance, so 'high performance sport has become the most popular dramatic representation of human achievement'. Fairchild (1994) suggests that such a description articulates a belief that 'elite sportspersons influence and shape our ideas of what we as human beings can and ought to be, what we ought to look like, and how we ought to behave'. This chapter, however, assesses practices by these modern icons of top level sport which fall far short of the ideal, and do not exemplify behaviour worthy of emulation.

All sports are social constructions – contrived or invented challenges set up to test the skills and ingenuity of the participants. Governing bodies are the guardians of what is considered to be the right and wrong ways to meet these challenges. These inventions – of right and wrong – are the arenas for the many ways in which sports practices are debased or corrupted. This chapter is about value-judgements by governing bodies and other commentators about what *ought* to happen in sports practices. For example, when playing sport, one ought not to take drugs, one ought not to cheat, one ought not to commit foul play ... because to do so, wrecks sport. In similar vein, Harper (1993) discusses 'just sport'. Just sport depends on both the adjectival and adverbial senses of the word. Sport ought to be both *fair* (just) and *only* (just) sport. He writes:

> Whoever enters the sports world and is obligated to accept the restrictions of sport's inherent code of fair play, and by playing it so, perpetuates the idea of playing sport for sport's sake.

However, such value-judgements are, at least implicitly, questioned in intensely competitive modern sport. The opening chapter argued that the source of most contemporary problems in sport arise from the irreducible tension between sport as a social practice (where internal goods are valued) and sport as a social institution (where external goods are valued). Internal goods, arising from the experiences of participation and valuing the sports **process** as an end in itself, are open to corruption when people value sports for ulterior motives, for particular **outcomes**.

Earlier chapters have examined this dynamic between processes and outcomes by documenting some of the recent pressures upon sports practices, notably a trend towards:

1 An **instrumental rationality** where an interest in outcomes supersedes an interest in process, and where an 'amateur' approach becomes inappropriate and unsustainable.
2 A **market rationality** where groups seek to make a profit from sports by tinkering with their structures and organization, to make them more spectacular and more consumer-friendly. As a widespread social practice with a massive and growing global audience, sports are open to political as well as economic exploitation.

Gruneau (1983) observes that these social, economic and political forces have resulted in a new **social definition** (i.e. a generally accepted and acknowledged set of understandings) of sport, intimately associated with professionalism both in terms of financial remuneration for a variety of sports roles, and in terms of the attitude appropriate for participation. In this environment, amateurism becomes an outmoded ideal, anachronistic and backward-looking. Contrary to the main tenets of amateurism, this new social definition creates an environment which encourages the corruption of sports practices through institutional pressures.

Most sports people are aware of issues such as violence by and among players, drug-taking, blood-doping, overt rule-breaking such as professional fouls, covert forms of cheating, and other practices which fly in the face of the doctrine of 'fair play'. Such activity detracts from the positive image of sport, and therefore hinders developmental strategies, particularly among impressionable youth. Consequently, many governing bodies have **fair play** initiatives high on their agenda, and awards for fair play are currently available in many sports and at all levels of performance.

Before considering the ways in which sports are corrupted and the responses of sports organizations, it is useful to recall the analysis in Chapter 1 of the social dynamics of sports processes. It was noted that sports inherently involve three sets of social relationships; namely cooperation, contest and association. The last of these is critical with respect to corrupting sport.

Association refers to inter-group collaboration – between individuals, groups or teams. Each and every participant in a sport *must* collaborate in this way in order to put the sport into practice. All must enter into a (usually informal) **contract** to participate and compete, and agree to join an internally and externally controlled system as given by the codified rules and procedures of the sport. This applies not only to the players or participants, but also to supportive and advisory personnel such as coaches, trainers and managers. Participants are, in effect, performing functions for one another, while seeking to maximize their own chances of success in meeting the sporting challenge.

Refusal by a player to **cooperate** or **contest** means being a 'spoilsport', but refusal to **associate** is far more serious. A win-at-all-costs approach to sport, instances of cheating, the use of performance-enhancing substances, are all examples of tipping the balance of social dynamics towards the interest in contest, and away from an interest in association. **The corruption of sports processes is, therefore, evidence of what might usefully be termed dis-association.**[1]

As an analytical framework, a distinction can be made between **contest problems** to denote dis-associating in the actual playing of sports, and **pre-contest problems**, which arise from processes in training and preparing for sports. Each of these will be examined before assessing the typical responses by sports organizations aimed at addressing these problems.

Types of disassociation: contest problems

All contest problems articulate around a con-sideration of the rules of a sport. Break these, and sports are corrupted. The rules provide a sport's virtual structure, give meaning to the playing processes and to winning and losing, and 'constitute' the practice. Contest problems can be unpacked by considering:

- the letter and the spirit of the rules
- intentional and unintentional rule violations
- overt and covert intentional rule violations.

---

[1] Elias and Dunning (1986) provide a detailed account of the social dynamics of sports, employing a figurational perspective. They outline ten 'tension-balances' or 'polarities in modern sports processes'. Upset any of these, and sport will be spoilt.

Letter and spirit of the rules

Fraleigh (1984) suggests that the constitutive rules include the:

- specific state of affairs to be achieved by the contestants
- means used to achieve a specific goal
- permitted equipment and materials to be used
- scoring or judging system
- regulations which, if violated, specify a prescribed penalty.

But Fraleigh goes further to make a distinction between the explicit **letter** and the implicit but, nevertheless crucial, **spirit** of the rules. Consider the following example from golf:

> The letter of a rule is what the rule states explicitly, or its legal sports substance. For example, the rule states that golf participants will execute their stroke from where the ball lies on the golf course, that they will hit the ball from where they have previously hit the ball to. The letter of this rule states, positively, to play the shots as they lie and, negatively, that improving one's lie is prohibited except under clearly specified exceptions. This is all the rule says explicitly. However, what is not explicitly stated but nonetheless it is a very real dimension of the same rule is its spirit.
>
> The spirit of sports rule is not what the rule states specifically, rather, it is the reason why the rules-makers made that particular rule a constitutive rule. Concerning the golf rule, the spirit of that rule is to reward previously good shots (such as balls hit into the middle of the fairway) and to penalise poor shots (such as balls hit into the rough, behind trees, etc.). The spirit of the rule assures that every golfer in the contest plays under conditions that reflect, equally for all, the quality of his previous shots and provides an equally good or poor lie, in principle, from which the players hit their next shots.
>
> If the participants understand only the letter of the rule, they have a limited base from which to determine how to follow the rules. Improving a golf lie may seem an innocent act to a contestant who does not comprehend the spirit of the rule. But when he knows that the spirit is absolutely

essential to a fair contest, he has something more than the letter to guide appropriate action. For the good sports contest, comprehending the letter and the spirit of constitutive rules is meant for everybody and for the good of everyone alike because it helps assure that all are facing the same test and, thus, are contesting.
(*Source*: Fraleigh (1984) by permission)

The distinction is critical because the explicit (i.e. codified) rules do not, and indeed cannot, precisely determine behaviour. There are always grey areas which allow for sports participants to make individual choices about how the rules are to be interpreted in a given situation. Therefore, the explicit rules rely upon performers collectively agreeing to abide by a code of conduct conventionally termed the spirit of the rules. Indeed, for many years the laws of soccer contained the phrase 'ungentlemanly conduct' in recognition of this facet of rules, this quality of 'association' in sports. It is evident that, in sport governed by an instrumental rationality, such niceties are lost!

But in some sports, the 'spirit' of the rules might mean actually breaking the letter of the rules. D'Agostino (1981) contends that every sport has an 'ethos' which denotes the unofficial and implicit conventions which determine how the formal rules (i.e. the 'letter') are to be applied. For example, basketball is replete with, or as D'Agostino has it, 'consists' of, bodily contact. Referees tacitly ignore violations of the contact rule since to do otherwise would destroy the viability of the game for both players and spectators. Rail (1990) makes similar points about basketball and draws a distinction between contacts which are perceived as 'good' (i.e. accidental or playful), and those which are perceived as 'bad' (i.e. violent), contacts. For example, hand-checking, screening and boxing-out are considered by both players and referees to be essential to basketball games and therefore are defined as playful. Similar points apply to sports like ice hockey. In some sports, therefore, certain rule violations are considered to be both a necessary and acceptable part of the game by both referees and players and are not, therefore, examples of disassociation from the contract to play or, therefore, contrary to the spirit of the rules.

Intentional and unintentional rule violations

Unintentional rule-breaking can occur by accident or because the participant is unaware of the rules. Accidental violations occur in every sport (e.g. off-side in soccer, overstepping the mark in triple jumping, touching the top of the net in volleyball). Also there are plenty of examples, even at the top level, of athletes claiming ignorance about the rules governing the allowable equipment or about banned medication. No problems arise from these as long as the activity is adequately policed to ensure that no undue advantage is gained. Governing bodies frequently make judgements about technological innovations (e.g. to javelins,to golf balls, to racing cars).

However, in some sports, athletes will commit intentional fouls but hope that they will be perceived as unintentional by the officials. For instance, collapsing a scrum in rugby union or 'accidentally' tripping and colliding with the ball-carrier in basketball. With respect to the latter example, a FIBA official and international referee has recently argued that the strategies in the final three minutes of the game hinge upon the referee's perception of whether fouls are intentional (personal fouls) or unintentional (technical fouls), for which different penalties are given (see Kew, 1987)! Conversely, feigning injury and constant complaining to the referee are used by some performers to create an impression that instances of fair play are made to look unfair and intentional fouls.

Overt and covert intentional rule violations

There are two kinds of intentional foul, only one of which can accurately be termed 'cheating'. Cheating is an intentional act when the athlete hopes not to be caught breaking the rules. At the Moscow Olympics, a Soviet fencer short-circuited the electronic scoring system so that he could register 'hits' at will. Ball-tampering in cricket, improving a golf lie and most 'off-the-ball' fouls in invasion games such as hockey, soccer or rugby are all examples of *covert* cheating.

The second kind of deliberate rule violation, this time *overt*, occurs when the athlete has calculated that s/he will be caught committing the offence, but reasons that some sort of tactical advantage will be gained by the offence. The so-called 'professional' foul in soccer is a good example. Rule-makers are constantly tinkering with sanctions to minimize a tactical advantage for the offending side from rule violations.

Typical responses to contest problems

Generally, the responses by various governing bodies of sport have fallen into the following categories which will be discussed in turn:

- more effective policing of the playing action
- more severe penalties
- changes to the rules
- educating players and coaches.

Policing and penalties

Electronic surveillance through video playbacks increases the power of referees and governing bodies to adjudicate about unfair play. Also, the increasing intensity of modern competitive sports has been paralleled by a corresponding increase in either the number of referees, umpires, linesmen, etc., or an increase in their powers. For example, the RFU now uses video evidence to suspend players for violence outside the laws of the game, and has also recently empowered linesmen to adjudicate on, and call the referee's attention to, off-the-ball instances of violent play.

Sports organizations also frequently tinker with the level of sanctions (e.g. penalties, direct/indirect free kicks, sin bins, yellow/red cards) to try to 'make the punishment fit the crime' and cleanse the sport of any advantage being gained from foul play. The FA, for example, now instructs referees to dismiss players for intentional fouls on opponents who have a clear opportunity to score a goal. Also, RFU referees make more frequent use of the penalty try.

Changes to the rules

As noted earlier, many rule changes are linked to the perceived need to make the sport more consumer-friendly and more spectacular. However, other rule changes are attempts by the rules committees of international governing bodies to respond to the devious ways in which players and coaches find of circumventing either or both the letter and spirit of the rules (see above) through the development of tactics. Evidence for this is clear in the chronic rule changes to specific elements of invasion games. Examples include successive changes to the offside, play-the-ball and scrummaging rules in Rugby League; the goalkeeping and offside rules in soccer; the line-out, scrummaging, kicking for touch, tackle and offside rules in Rugby Union.

One of these examples illustrates the case. The offside rule in soccer has been changed or modified in 1866, 1873, 1894, 1902, 1907, 1913, 1914, 1920, 1923, 1925, 1936 and 1988. Other changes that have been proposed or experimented with for short periods include:

no off-side in the penalty area; a 75-metre line for offside rather than the opponents' half of the field; no offside if the player is not intentionally seeking to gain an advantage or interfering with play; no offside if the ball is kicked from one's own half of the field; no offside from direct or indirect free kicks; no offside from goalkeepers' kicks; no offside at all.

Basketball offers a classic example of the problems facing rule makers. A recent FIBA official described the following rule changes as 'attempts to outwit the coaches' to ensure that the last three minutes of basketball matches are not completely spoilt. The chronology (Figure 4.1) spans the Los Angeles Olympics and its aftermath.

1 In 1984, after eight team fouls, subsequent fouls incurred the following penalty: one shot at the basket which, if successful, enabled another shot to be taken (i.e. 1+1). If the first shot was unsuccessful no further shot was allowed. Before 1984, there had been two shots on basket irrespective of whether the first missed or not. Hence the penalty for exceeding eight team fouls had been reduced (from 2 to 1+1).

2 When a foul is committed in the last three minutes, the clock is stopped. Coaches now began to instruct players (who had incurred few personal fouls – 5 are allowed), to immediately foul the player in possession of the ball. Result is 1+1 shots at basket **but** (a) only one or two seconds had elapsed, and (b) possession of the ball is regained by the offending side after the shots on basket.

3 This tactic is further refined. Coaches tell the players to guard the best opposing shooters so that they won't receive the ball, and to foul the poorest shooter as soon as he receives the ball. FIBA officials said that 'as a spectacle, as a fair contest, this was useless ... the last three minutes could last twenty minutes'.

4 New rule instituted in 1986. Intentional fouls (after eight team fouls) incur two free throws (an increase from 1+1) **plus** possession of the ball in mid-court. If the foul was **not** intentional, then the penalty incurred remains at 1+1 and possession to the offending side. But 'there's still a weakness in the rules because it still relies on the referee's perception that it was an intentional foul'. Referees are therefore instructed to be alert to the possibility of fouls being intentional.

5 The new strategy of coaches is to instruct players to commit intentional fouls **but** to make them appear unintentional; e.g. tripping up into an opposing player, etc. Hence tactics hinge upon the evaluation by the referee of the intentions of the players!

Figure 4.1 Basketball rules: the last three minutes
(*Source*: Kew, 1987)

Educating players and coaches

The Central Council of Physical Recreation (CCPR), the Sports Council and the National Coaching Foundation have produced guidelines and codes of conduct to instil an ethos of fair play among athletes. Governing bodies also produce 'Fair Play' booklets and include such considerations in training courses for coaches and players. The CCPR's 'Charter of Conduct' is of interest in counterposing a 'traditional British approach to sport' (which regards 'fair play', 'sportsmanship' and 'playing the game' as essential) with modern developments which undermine these values. They write:

> It is widely felt that standards of behaviour and conduct amongst competitors, spectators and commentators have declined; harmful practices have crept in on a scale that threaten to undermine the very purpose of sport as a beneficial form of individual and social recreation. Even more worrying is the baleful effect on the younger generation of the frequent examples of misconduct and malpractice in many popular spectator sports.

The 'Charter for Competitors' lists the following duties and responsibilities of all sports competitors. They:

1 Must abide by both the laws and the spirit of their sport.
2 Must accept the decisions of umpires and referees without question or protestation.
3 Must not cheat and in particular must not attempt to improve their performance by the use of drugs.
4 Must exercise self-control at all times.
5 Must accept success and failure, victory and defeat with good grace and without excessive display of emotion.
6 Must treat their opponents and fellow participants with due respect at all times.

The emphasis here is to shape attitudes towards competition by placing a high value on 'association', thereby promoting a positive image of sport. One would expect policy-making and politically sensitive organizations such as the CCPR to make statements to safeguard the integrity of sport, and individual sports faced with problems of 'disassociation' respond likewise. For example, ice hockey is full of, and perhaps consists of, rule violations. Vaz (1977) suggests that the inability of ice hockey to reduce rule violation is not inefficiency in rule-enforcement measures, but rather in the very structure of the rules. An increasingly punitive approach to reducing rule violations would jeopardize the viability of the game. So the answer is not heavier policing but education and re-socialization of players. He writes:

> Success according to game rules should be strongly emphasised and is in accord with the wider values of society. Players must be taught to want to obey the rules of the game. Thus both success and rule-obedience must be rewarded in the socialisation of hockey players.

Some might argue that both the CCPR charter and Vaz's educational approach to prevent rule-breaking are idealistic, and display little understanding of the complexities of the competitive process or of the pressures of intense elite competition. Other than contest problems, the intensity of modern competitive sport has resulted in corrupt and exploitative practices in preparation and training for performance; these might be termed **pre-contest** problems.

Types of disassociation: pre-contest problems

There are other instances of 'disassociation' when sportspersons, their coaches, trainers, managers and other supportive personnel attempt to gain an unfair advantage prior to, and in preparation for, sports contests. A well-publicized incidence of this is the various forms of blood-doping and use of banned performance-enhancing substances taken as part of training regimens. This might be with or without the knowledge of the athlete which itself raises ethical issues around self-advocacy. The British Olympic Association, the Sports Council's drug-testing unit and the British Association of Sports Medicine are at the forefront of both education and detection programmes.

Another problem is match-fixing, as has recently been disclosed in both French and British soccer. Less well-publicized are the attempts to exploit technological developments in equipment design and thereby gain an unfair advantage. Governing body regulations are continuously modified to take account of such developments.

Currently, of most concern is the growing acknowledgement that the intense and largely private preparation required for high levels of sports performance produces an environment where the minds and bodies of athletes can be manipulated, exploited and abused, especially by coaches and trainers.

The exploitation and abuse of athletes

Athletes, particularly at the highest levels, have little or no control over the wider context of their practice, or, indeed over the practice itself. Maguire (1991) argues that:

> Elite athletes can be viewed as workers who have little or no control over the product or the circumstances in which it is produced.... The consequence of this 'alienation process' is most evident when athletes become the producers of a system which then confronts and controls them.

Top athletes often have little control over training regimens, the strategies and styles of play adopted, the scheduling of events, the intensity and format of competitions, or the commercial exploitation of the fruits of their labour. Although applying particularly to the elite level, other levels of participation are not immune, since there is a marked tendency for lower level (e.g. youth sport) to emulate the training and playing styles of elite levels. Undue pressure is often put on children by parents who perhaps are revisiting their own thwarted ambition in sport.

With respect to coaching, the relationship with athletes is essentially one of trust and crucially, of power – both of which can be abused, especially in an environment which demands a wholesale commitment to raising levels of performance. Coaches can exert power over training regimens, competitive schedules, diet, dress, social contacts and lifestyle generally. The incidence of abusive coach/athlete relationships is confirmed in Yorganci's (1992) survey of 149 Scottish athletes. Table 4.1 documents the percentage of female athletes who had experienced intrusive influences from their coach in this survey.

Table 4.1 The influence of coaches on female athletes

Aspects	Percentage of female athletes
Diet/weight	56
Sleep	27
Dress code	17
Hair style	10
Social life/parties	30
Boyfriends/sex life	14

Yorganci also found that 54% of respondents had experienced or knew someone who had experienced at least one of the following elements of sexual harassment: demeaning language including sexual innuendo, unwarranted invitations, intrusive physical contact, fondling the genital area, pressure to have sexual intercourse from their coach or other performers. While very few experience the more extreme forms of sexual harassment, the recent conviction of an Olympic swimming coach for systematically indecently assaulting and/or raping 15 girl swimmers over a period of 15 years is instructive. Two commentaries on this case provide some explanation of why this abuse continued without discovery for so long. The first is by one of the victims who, instead of reporting the offender, had tried mentally to block out the physical and sexual attacks:

> They would have taken my swimming away from me and that was really important to me. I just felt pathetic, ashamed, embarrassed and ugly. I had been emotionally and physically raped at an age when I trusted others.

The second commentary comes from the prosecutor in the court case:

> It is a classic case of a person in authority, or in a position of trust, abusing that trust. Most endured his conduct over months and even years. They tolerated his behaviour in the knowledge that to displease him or break the links would adversely affect their career. Some were frightened of him.

The dominant themes in these two statements are the power and control exerted by an older, male coach over the younger female swimmers, together with the trust invested in the perpetrator of the abuse. Drawing upon French and Raven's (1959) analysis of social power, Brackenridge (1991) argues that the following sources of power are available to the coach:

Reward power — power over rewards
Coercive power — power to force someone
Legitimate power — power by virtue of senior rank
Expert power — power of knowledge and expertise
Charismatic power — power based on affection, infatuation or charisma.

Such sources of power are not in themselves abusive, but as Brackenridge suggests, abuse arises where there is 'invasion of body or psychological space without consent'. Current research into this sensitive topic reveals that abusive and exploitative relationships are most likely to occur:

- with younger athletes, especially but not exclusively in those individual sports where optimum performance is reached at an early age (e.g. gymnastics, swimming);
- where men coach women/girls.

Brackenridge draws together these two issues of age and gender to provide a profile (Table 4.2) of the balance of power between male coaches and female athletes.

Table 4.2 Power profile: male coach/female athlete

	Male Coach	*Female Athlete*
Age	Older	Younger
Knowledge of sport	Extensive	Limited
Size/physique	Large/strong	Small
Traditional authority	Superior	Subordinate
Control over selection/destiny	Much	Little/none

Source: Brackenridge (1991), by permission.

A case study of abuse and exploitation

In what follows there is no implication that this case study is representative of most athlete/coach relationships in Britain or elsewhere. Nevertheless, these excerpts from a real-life account of one athlete's experiences in sport over a five-year period provide a graphic illustration of systematic abuse of this person's commitment and abilities in athletics. She agreed to this account being published to increase awareness of problems experienced by some young athletes, and to encourage all those who have power over young sportspeople to adopt a code of conduct supportive of the interests of young athletes. Several elements of abusive and exploitative practice are illustrated in the extracts from her account, in particular:

- coach's employment dependent upon the relative success of his athletes
- control and surveillance over lifestyle
- abuse of the body, overtraining, training with injuries
- sexual harassment, sexual 'favours'
- substance abuse
- psychological problems, burn-out
- ultimate rejection of sport.

I was recruited on a full athletic scholarship by a coach from the university. Ultimately, I was to discover that this coach's contract was dependent upon the Track and Field team being successful. Negative performances would inhibit the renewal of the coach's contract. So the pressures and stress on the coach were reflected in his treatment of athletes.

I agreed to a scholarship for sprinting, sprint hurdling, and long jump.... On arrival, these conditions were revoked. My abilities were abused in that I was utilized in all aspects; e.g. 400 metres, cross-country, 1500 metres.... At the impressionable age of 18, with a previously sheltered lifestyle, I was thrust into an environment of strictly enforced regulations. We had to internalize philosophies and make them part of us. As a group of athletes we seemed to lose our personal freedom and identity, and experienced a loss of privacy. Typical doctrinaire slogans included:

- If you are willing to put in the work and sacrifice, you will improve.
- Keep your goals constantly in mind and do not let anything get in your way. Your number one goal should be to continue to perform and improve and enjoy what you are doing.
- When you set your goals, you have to internalize them. Make them part of you.

We had to keep a diary of a very personal nature which was to be submitted to the coach twice weekly. It was an extension of the mind, body and personal goals. It was to record psychological ups and downs; sleep hours and times you went to bed; diet – eating properly; weight; any physical ailments. This the coach examined and commented upon, and would often reply with criticisms like: 'You've got to lose 3 pounds before the week is out'.

Having gone to the university with no foundation training and reached national ranking within the top three juniors without any training facilities, I was put into a regime of training three times a day, six days a week and competing on the seventh day. For training sessions we had to be up by 6 a.m. to do a distance or water work-out and have our daily weigh-in; followed by morning academic lectures. I often missed lunch due to training sessions between 1 and 4 p.m. If we were not punctual, then we were reprimanded. There was hardly enough time to eat. Then further lectures, dinner between 5.30 and 6 p.m., then a couple of hours' study, then weight training between 8 and 9.30 p.m, followed by further study. I found it difficult to relax much at all. I went to bed at 1–2 a.m and got very little sleep.

I regularly resorted along with my room-mate to a caffeine stimulant at night to complete the heavy work-load – thus I rarely slept. Subsequently at training I often experienced shaking and diarrhoea. I eventually developed colitis and had a very low white blood cell count. I was exhausted after the training. In the first three months of training, I suffered from extreme fatigue and depression; but at the same time I was running very fast in time-trials. My coach was excited and would often take me out for meals and talk about my potential. My coach was so keen on my potential that he devoted a lot of personal attention on me. So much so, that the coach became an extension of my mind and body.'

(There then followed a time of injury and intensive rehabilitation.)

Despite the surgeon's advice, I began intensive training again with my coach and my performance showed rapid progression. It was decided I would be ready for the forth-coming championships. My training became more intense and as a result my leg gave way again only 9 months after the first injury (the metal staple had worked loose and the artificial ligaments had become detached, damaging the bone).

I now came under pressure to abort my education half-way through the course, with the threat of losing my sports scholarship. As an attempt to numb the pain of my athletics, I rigorously immersed myself in my academic study which won me academic recognition, to be awarded an academic scholarship.

(After second surgery, and under pressure from the coach, she began training again.)

Again, because of my conservative nature, I found the lack of privacy, and the regulations to which I was forced to comply, completely abhorrent. Despite time trials of PB runs and a few competitions, my motivation was waning. I found myself suffering from depression and eating disorders, as were 80% of the team, due to the stress of maintaining an ideal training weight imposed by the coach.

Being a sprinter, and naturally having a muscular body composition, I was finding it extremely difficult with the intense weight training to maintain a stable weight. I resorted to anorexic and bulemic tendencies which eventually became an established way of maintaining weight. Some days, if I was tired in training, I would be told it was due to lack of effort and as a punishment made to do a session of e.g. 20 by 400 metres with no recovery at literally 100% until you dropped from exhaustion. This was a test beyond any recognition of human limits.

On travelling to competitions at weekends, the coach would allocate people to certain rooms, with athletes having no choice about whom they shared with. Sometimes, certain athletes had to occupy just a single room and the coach would invite himself in on the premise of giving a pre-meeting build up, involving a pep talk and physical preparation including a 'sensual massage' for relaxation. In return, the athlete was expected to oblige the coach with a similar but more explicit favour. My scholarship for the year was dependent upon my relationship with the coach. Therefore it was a form of emotional blackmail due to the sexual appetite and the obsessive body image of the coach. I reached a point where the pressure became too great.

(She eventually terminated her scholarship and came home).

> At present, I have chosen to neglect organized sport and pursue a 'caring' approach to recreation for disadvantaged, non-competitive groups of people. My energies and enthusiasms are now geared towards achieving in an academic field. I keep fit by testing my individual limits in events such as cycling, hiking, rock-climbing. Often I will do ultra-endurance runs at night when feeling stressed. I don't enjoy them, but I feel maybe it is a way of punishing myself and pushing myself to the limit in an activity my body type is not suited for.

Responses to exploitation

Monitoring

A recent study carried out by the Sports Council and the Institute of Child Health, recognizing the potential physical and psychological damage of heavy training during adolescence, aims to keep teenagers off the sacrificial altar of early success. Over 500 young athletes are involved in the study.

Gymnasts have been screened for spinal injuries and delayed menarche, swimmers for skin disorders, sleeping difficulties and ear, nose and throat problems, soccer players for leg injuries and behavioural disorders, and tennis players for arm injuries and sleeping problems.

In addition to over-use injuries, the study aims to uncover evidence of disrupted social family and school life, and in parents and coaches who put too much psychological pressure on the young athletes. Further, national governing bodies are now asked to investigate the conditions of training and coaching for young athletes.

Empowerment

For Coakley (1992), such monitoring does not go far enough in understanding the social conditions of young elite athletes and their experience of growing up, or in understanding 'burn-out' – a social phenomenon in which many young people drop out of sport. The tennis players Andrea Jaeger, Tracy Austen and most recently, Jennifer Capriati, are perhaps the most well-publicized examples. According to Coakley, burn-out arises because of two factors: (a) a limited set of life-experiences and the formation of a personal identity restricted to their sports role, and (b) power relationships in and around sport, notably with parents and coaches, which restricts the amount of personal control young athletes have over their lives. Unlike other teenagers who can try out, experiment with and nurture a number of different identities, the sports experience of high level young athletes involves, as Coakley (1992) says:

> ... social experiences that fostered the development of a single identity exclusively related to sports participation and perpetuated a limited set of social relationships directly tied to sport. The people in their lives continuously responded to them in terms of their specialised sports roles, their time was almost exclusively devoted to the development of specialised skills, and their goals were well-defined and tied to assumptions of commitment to long-term specialised sports training.... For them, sport involvement became analagous to being on a tightrope; it was exciting, they were good, they were the centre of attention, but they knew they couldn't shift their focus to anything else without losing their balance, they knew there would be no net to catch them.

Coakley's solution is to create an environment where the athletes feel more in control of their sports participation, where dependency on coaches or parents is reduced, and where athletes are empowered to make decisions about the direction of their own development. This 'empowerment' model of practice is to include:

- jointly established performance goal-setting
- encouragement to take part in social events and develop interests outside the sports setting

- encouragement to ask critical questions about their own sports involvement
- allowing athletes to find their own solutions to sports problems.

Codes of conduct for coaches

Most of the above sentiments are enshrined in the codes of conduct for coaches drawn up by the CCPR, the NCF and others. Codes of conduct befitting the professions are nothing new, and the growing professionalization of the coaching role makes this inevitable. The British Institute of Sports Coaches (BISC) code of conduct includes three key points with respect to athletes' rights. Coaches:

1 Must respect the rights, dignity and worth of every performer and their ultimate right to self-determination. Everyone must be treated equally regardless of sex, ethnic origin, religion, or political persuasion.
2 Should be concerned primarily with the well-being, health and future of the individual and only secondarily with the optimization of performance.
3 Should encourage performers to accept responsibility for their own behaviour and performance in training, in competition, and in their social life, to make autonomous choices about their involvement in sport.

A critical note: individual or system?

Typical responses to both contest and pre-contest problems are aimed at individual athletes or teams. These consist of a range of measures to re-educate, to impose sanctions and to develop heavier policing and surveillance, whether of sports contests or athletes' lifestyles. However, is it as simple as focusing attention on the individual miscreants? The opening chapter discussed the tension between the social practice and the social institution of sport, and it is institutional or systemic pressures which encourage individuals to corrupt the practice of sport. To illustrate this, let us examine one well-documented case of corrupting sports practice – the drug-abuse by an international athlete, the sprinter Ben Johnson.[2]

The Individual
In one sense the corruption of sports practices is, of course, a result of individual actions. The player cheats, commits professional fouls, takes drugs. The coach abuses and exploits athletes. The parent puts unwarranted pressure on the child to realize his/her own (thwarted) sporting ambition. Players need to be educated or re-socialized to obey the rules in letter and spirit. Referees and umpires are instructed to increase sanctions on rule violators. Coaches are instructed not to manipulate rules in the interests of their charges. Players and coaches are asked to re-affirm their commitment to certain ethical standards of behaviour in sport. Governing bodies conduct training courses and seminars to implement accept-able practice. All this in the interest of protecting the integrity of sports practice.

The system
However, it is instructive to analyse the environment or networks in which an athlete like Ben Johnson is operating. Table 4.3 maps out in simple form the various groups in elite sports production and gives an account of their interests in such activity.

---

[2] Heikkala (1991) addresses the 'doping dilemma' among elite athletes who have to reconcile the perceived tension between self-interest and communality. He writes: 'The rationality for competing does not support the co-operation needed for the proposed solution (to doping).'

Table 4.3 Top sport: networks of production

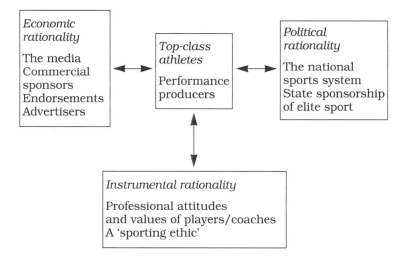

It has already been established that sports are subject to both a market rationality and to an instrumental rationality, and that this eventuates in the corruption of sports practices. In practical terms, how does this relate to the case of Ben Johnson, or indeed any other top-flight sportsperson?

Taking the elements of Table 4.3 in turn, the media devote an almost exclusive attention on the winners in sport, especially an event with the global coverage of the Olympics. This, in turn, makes the winners marketable commodities for commercial interests, illustrated by the fact that most top sportspeople make more money out of commercial activity than out of competing. A gold medallist at the Olympics, particularly in a high-profile event like the 100 metres, stands to make millions out of endorsing products, advertising, television shows, and celebrity appearances.

Coupled with this economic interest is the political interest of the nation state. Canada, (Johnson's home country) like other Western industrialized nations, has constructed a national sports system (Sports Canada) whose explicit objective is the creation of sporting excellence. This system, part of the political dynamic of the country, invests in high-quality sports performers by focusing technical expertise, financial resources and training facilities on their preparation for international competition.

A sport's governing body is part of this system and coaches, in effect, are charged with implementing the programme to create successful international athletes. Hughes and Coakley (1991), in an article entitled 'Positive deviance amongst athletes', give some insights about what this involves in terms of the commitment of performers. They argue that top athletes **over-conform** to the sporting ethic. At this level, marginal improvements in performance can mean all the difference between winning and losing. Being an athlete involves making sacrifices, striving for distinction, accepting risks and playing through pain, not backing down from challenges or refusing to accept limits in the pursuit of possibilities. 'No pain, no Spain' – the motto of athletes at a training camp for the Barcelona Olympics.

Finally, the status and prestige of Johnson's coach and other supportive personnel is inevitably linked to their ability to produce winners which, as we noted earlier, can lead to an exploitative relationship. This then is the environment for the production of sports performances which encourages an instrumental rationality. All available resources of time, money, technical and medical knowledge and expertise are brought to bear to produce excellence.

Who then is to blame for corrupting sports practices? Certainly it is *individuals* – in this case an athlete taking banned substances – who break the rules and regulations, but their actions need to be seen in a broader context. The *system* of sports production, involving the various economic, political and professional interest groups, creates conditions within which it sometimes makes sense to corrupt the sports practice if such action goes undetected. Media interests, commercial interests, the national organization for creating sporting excellence, the positions of coaches and other advisers within these organizations are all geared up to celebrate winners. Simultaneously, sports organizations issue codes of conduct which retreat from this instrumental rationality to focus upon the internal goods of sports practice, on the rights of athletes to self-determination, on a socially acceptable image of uncorrupted sports practice – images which are in the interest of the media and commerce to sustain.

There are then two seemingly irreconcilable forces at work within the system of sports production. One provides rewards and status to successful sporting outcomes (winning), and the other castigates those individuals who try to achieve these outcomes through deviant means and by doing so 'disassociate' themselves from sport. To repeat, **the system creates the very conditions which encourage the corruption of sports practices**.[3]

---

[3] The reader is referred back to the more extensive analysis of the relationship between sports practice and sports institution in Chapter 1.

Part Two

Sport and Structural Inequality

In a recent article in 'The Times' newspaper, Libby Purves celebrated individualism, human differences and capacities, which throw our preconceptions into confusion. Citing, among others, the example of the 'burly Geordie track engineer with British Rail who had trained as a court dress-maker', she stated that:

> ... nobody's inwardness can be accurately predicted by age, sex, class, or physical type' ... we are alive, we are diverse, our minds soar above and beyond the matter we are made of.... We have changed our laws and social customs so that the old stereotypes are banned: you can no longer condemn your neighbour for living over the brush or being black, nor make assumptions about women, or Welshmen, or people with a limp (though it is still OK to insult the middle class) ... in practice we cling more desperately than ever to any handle we can get, from Basildon Man to Executive Tart. I hate these as much as the old stereotypes: people who peddle them do more damage than they know. They are like Victorian butterfly collectors, happiest when their subject is pinned out dead.... Typecasting is a blunt instrument and a dangerously tempting one.

Libby Purves' argument is, I argue, both right and wrong. She is right to point out that there *are* laws in place which render discriminatory practices with respect to race, sex and disability illegal. She is also right to argue that individuals do *not* necessarily conform to stereotypes and do transcend and minimize the effects of discriminatory social conditions.

An important element of Part Two of this book is to challenge stereotypical assumptions about disabled people, black people, women, men. Whether white/black, young/old, men/women, able-bodied/ disabled, blue collar/white collar workers, people *do* make informed choices on the basis of the opportunities available to them ... in sport and leisure or other spheres of their lives. Hence, there *are* women in top management positions, black ballet dancers, disabled people who scale mountains, house-husbands ... just to add a few to Purves' list of examples which do not conform to stereotypes. This is indeed an important corrective to blinkered analysis which forefronts **social structure** as a determining influence on behaviour at the expense of **agency** and **choice**.

However, Purves goes further and seems to be preaching, and indeed celebrating, a brand of individualism which is negated by much social research. Probably, social research would be an obvious target for Libby Purves. Academic and institutional arrangements in the various branches of sociology are often contoured by what she might deride as stereotypical thinking. There are courses in Women's Studies, Caribbean Studies, South Asian Studies, and discourses around age, social class, disability, each of which forefront a particular social condition as the basis of subsequent analysis, as an explanation of difference and inequity, and as a rationale for political intervention in a bid for power and resources.

Sociologists *do* argue, contra to Purves, and to Margaret Thatcher's oft-quoted assertion 'that there is no such thing as society', that social processes (including sports) *are* structured through crucial and recognizable divisions between people which translate into differences and inequalities in life-chances. The sociology of sport is no exception and this section is organized with respect to, arguably, the most important of these social divisions.

Social class, gender, ethnicity and disability are salient factors in understanding inequality (i.e.

unequal) and inequity (i.e. unfairness) with respect to opportunities for sport. Many of these social factors have a biological basis. Age, sex, race, and mental and physical abilities, are relatively unproblematic ways of distinguishing between people. Yet, it is important to consider a social dimension to these factors. For example, in biological terms, ageing is a process of birth, growth and development, degeneration and death. In social terms, societies reconstruct these inevitable biological processes, to give them meaning and significance; e.g. stages such as childhood, adolescence, or its equivalent, middle and old age, and critical life-events such as menarche, marriage, the birth of children, death. Similarly, sex has a biological basis, but gender is a social construction in so far as value and significance is placed upon sexual difference.

Race, gender, class, and disability have a profound, if not determining, influence upon individuals, upon institutions such as sport and upon social relations generally. In subsequent chapters, most of the issues about sport articulate around:

- stereotypical images of groups of people and the consequences for sport
- an imbalance of power and resources between groups
- a lack of control over the organization and practice of sport.

The following extract from Critcher *et al.* (1995) provides an apt introduction to the following four chapters:

> The first step is to acknowledge that class, gender, and race are crucial ingredients in social relations, both as resources and constraints. The next step is to try to explain how these differences of class, gender, and race are in turn mediated by people's experiences and social practices.

Sport, racism and ethnicity

Multiculturalism

Britain is a multicultural society. For centuries, people have come to this country in search of work or employment, a better quality of life, or as refugees from political, racial or religious persecution; for example, immigrants from Eastern Europe (e.g. Ukrainians, Latvians, Lithuanians, Poles, Estonians, Hungarians) and also Italians, Spaniards, Greeks, Chinese, Malays, Kenyans, German Jews, etc. Many of these people have sought to sustain a separate cultural identity at a distance from the indigenous culture of Britain. However, the most common connotations of multiculturalism in Britain focus upon groups from South Asia (India, Pakistan, Bangladesh, Sri Lanka) and from the former British colonies in the Caribbean, who form the largest ethnic minorities in Britain.

The Sports Council takes this narrower (i.e. non-white) definition of 'ethnic minorities' to state that the population of these groups had risen from less than 1% in 1951 to approximately 5.5% by 1990. The geographical distribution is uneven, with 70% of the non-white population concentrated in the four metropolitan areas of Greater London, West Midlands, West Yorkshire and Greater Manchester. The age structure is different from the white population with over 60% under the age of 30, as compared with only 43% in the population as a whole. At the other end of the age spectrum, only about 5% of non-white groups are over 60, compared with over 20% of the general population. Of the current Black Caribbean community, 53% were born in the UK, most of whom, according to Fryer (1993), call themselves 'Black British'.

Within each of these four localities there is considerable ethnic diversity. For example, in Bradford, West Yorkshire, ward profiles reveal that South Asians in the district of Manningham are predominantly Pakistanis from the Punjab region. A few miles away, Keighley has a large Bangladeshi community, originally from a predominantly rural, working class background in the southern delta region. Table 5.1 provides some population figures.

Table 5.1 Resident population by ethnic group: Great Britain, 1991

Ethnic group	No. ('000)	Percentage of total population	Percentage of total ethnic minority population
White	51 874	94.5	
Ethnic minorities	3015	5.5	100
Black groups	891	1.6	29.5
Black Caribbean	500	0.9	16.6
Black African	212	0.4	7.0
Black Other	178	0.3	5.9
Indian	840	1.5	27.9
Pakistani	477	0.9	15.8
Bangladeshi	163	0.3	5.4
Chinese	157	0.3	5.2
Other groups			
Asian	198	0.4	6.6
non-Asian	290	0.5	9.6

Source: OPCS 1991 Census, pub.1993; the first to include a question on ethnic groups.

Ideally, multiculturalism suggests a recognition of cultural diversity without using the values of one culture to judge the worth of another. This level of tolerance and consequent absence of an **ethnocentric** perspective is difficult to achieve, and the practice and organization of sport is but one area of culture which falls short of the ideal. This chapter considers different dimensions of racism before addressing the experience of Afro-Caribbeans and South Asians in Britain.

Racism

Historically, race has been used by scientists and ethnologists who attempt to categorize people on the basis of physical appearance and other inherited characteristics. The biological theories on which early race theory was based in the nineteenth century have largely been discarded (although, notoriously, racial differences in intelligence is still researched), especially as these theories were used to justify slavery and the exploitation of black people by white. As noted later, biological explanations of sports performance are still expounded, and are subject to sociological critique.

The concept of **racism** is used with reference to societies (including British) in which one 'racial' group is in a position of dominance over others. Racism entails a body of ideas which rationalizes and justifies various social practices that perpetuate an unequal distribution of power between racial groups. In essence, *racism = prejudice + power* and there is continuing evidence of racism in the practice and organization of sport. Three interdependent dimensions of racism are worth identifying – structural, institutional and individual.

Structural
Economic and social discrimination against black people is embedded in the structure of society, as evidenced in employment, housing and education. In Britain, an immigrant population was recruited in the postwar economic boom to combat labour shortages primarily in the manufacturing sector, resulting in relatively low pay, social conditions and life-choices for these groups. Thirty-five per cent of Bangladeshis

are unemployed, 11.8% of Indians and 19% of black Caribbeans, compared with only 10% of whites.

Institutional

Institutions maintain sets of rules and/or procedures and practices which operate in ways to perpetuate discrimination against black people. This chapter provides evidence of sport's contribution to this, but it occurs in other areas such as education, the arts, the legal system and the media.

Individual

The actions and attitudes of individuals to black people support and reproduce social problems of discrimination. Examples of *overt* racism at this individual level includes 'Paki-bashing', racist taunts from football terraces, and some commonly-held assumptions about innate sporting prowess of some racial groups. Individual racism might also be *tacit* or unacknowledged; taken-for-granted commonsense assumptions about the attributes of groups on the basis of race. Although few regard themselves as 'racist', there are over 140 000 racially-motivated attacks in the UK every year.

Black representation in British sport

One might reasonably argue that sport (unlike various professions such as the arts and law) is one of the few elements of culture which is accessible to ethnic minorities, providing an avenue for upward social mobility. This is graphically illustrated (Table 5.2) in a survey carried out in October 1992 by the 'Weekly Journal' – a newspaper aimed at Britain's black and Asian communities. This survey provides a list of the twenty wealthiest black people in Britain. *Note that six of the top eleven are sportsmen (no women!) and that these sportsmen are all Afro-Caribbean not South Asian, which indicates differences in the place of sport within their respective cultures.*

Table 5.2 The wealthiest black people in Britain

		Wealth (£m)	Occupation
1	Kojo Owusu Nyantekyi	20	Industrialist
2	Frank Bruno	5.5	Boxer
3	Shirley Bassey	5.2	Singer
4	Sade Adu	5	Singer
5	John Barnes	4	Footballer
6	Joan Armatrading	4	Musician
7	Des Walker	3.5	Footballer
8	Billy Ocean	3	Musician
9	John Fashanu	3	Footballer
10	Chris Eubank	2.6	Boxer
11	Linford Christie	2.4	Athlete
12	Naomi Campbell	2.3	Model
13	Winston Isaacs	2	Hairdresser
14	Val McCalla	2	Publisher
15	Clem Rodney	1.5	Entrepreneur
16	Dyke & Dryden	1	Cosmetics
17	Anthony Gee	1	Jeweller
18	Maxi Priest	1	Musician
19	Douanne Alexander Moore	1	Food producer
20	Jazzie B	0.75	Musician

Accepted uncritically, this list may suggest that racism is not an important issue and there is no demonstrable need for anti-racist strategies or positive action! There are plenty of black people in sports such as soccer, boxing and athletics which suggests that sport is one of the few areas of social life free from racism. Or is it?

Survey findings show that black people, both men and women, are *under*-represented in many sports (e.g. golf, tennis, swimming, outdoor pursuits) but are *over*-represented in other sports (e.g. athletics, basketball, men's soccer). For example, Afro-Caribbeans comprise only 1.6% of the total population but 7.7% (and rising) of the total number of professional soccer players. In contrast, how many black British men/women golf or tennis players, swimmers, gymnasts, snooker players, can you identify? South Asian men are over-represented in hockey and badminton, but under-represented in soccer and rugby.

This raises a number of questions. Why are patterns of involvement in sport uneven across the range of sports? Is there an inequality of access and opportunity for some sports? Are some racial groups innately better/worse at different sports? Is an explanation for under-representation and over-representation to be found in terms of the three dimensions of racism identified previously? How far do sports organizers, teachers and coaches collude with, and actively perpetuate, discriminatory practices?

The Afro-Caribbean experience

Racism is not limited to overt expressions of racial abuse which surface, for example, on the football terraces, or in the perjorative implications of comments such as 'niggers', 'Pakis', 'coons'; or in the well-publicized stereotyping, by chairmen of soccer clubs, that blacks are skilful players but less effective in the mud and rain of a British winter! A survey by a leading black newspaper, 'The Voice', showed that over half of the respondents refused to support the two British soccer teams in Euro 96. The outpouring of nationalism tinged with xenophobia resonated too well with their own daily lived experience. Should England have won, they feared it would be never-ending. They preferred to support those teams who had most black players such as Holland and France.

The main thrust of research into racism in sport (e.g. Cashmore, 1982, 1991; Carrington, 1983; Leaman and Carrington, 1985; Jarvie, 1990) is to examine its **ideological** and **institutional** dimensions; more precisely how racial stereotyping systematically 'channels' blacks, and how sport serves to perpetuate and reinforce racial inequality. Sport might be an avenue of upward social mobility, but only for the very few! Fleming (1994) reviews Nugent and King's (1979) outline of the process of stereotyping. This involves three stages:

- the identification of a category of people, e.g. blacks, estate agents
- the attribution of traits to that category
- the application of these traits to anyone and everyone who belongs to that category.

This process is abundantly clear with respect to some widely-held beliefs about the innate prowess of Afro-Caribbeans in sport relative to whites.

Biologism: 'natural' ability

The conventional wisdom about black success in sport is rooted in biology. In a nutshell this 'wisdom' is that black's (i.e. Afro-Caribbean's) performance in sport can be explained by innate anatomical, physiological and psychological characteristics which gives them inbuilt advantage in some sports and a disadvantage in others (e.g. swimming). Why else, for example, should 80% of Olympic finalists in the 100 metres for men over the last 20 years be black? Why else should there have been no white heavyweight boxing champions of the world since Rocky Marciano? Why else should there be hardly any black swimming champions? This 'natural ability' perspective has some powerful supporters both within the hierarchy of many governing bodies of sport and in biological research, as Cashmore (1982) demonstrates in his critique of Kane's (1971) explanation of black success in sport.

Kane constructs three key arguments for black success, namely physiological, psychological and historical. The *physiological* argument is that blacks are genetically better equipped physically and physiologically for sport. Coakley (1986) elaborates upon this reasoning by reviewing a number of similar studies which have had the following conclusions:

1 The bodies of blacks are proportionally different than those of whites. They have longer legs and arms, shorter trunks, less body fat, more slender hips, more tendon and less muscle, a different heel structure, wider calf bones, more slender calf muscles, greater arm circumference, and more of the muscle fibres needed for speed and power and fewer of those needed for endurance.
2 The bodies of blacks function differently from the bodies of whites ... they mature more rapidly, their lung capacity is lower, they are more likely to have hyper-extensibility ... they dissipate heat more efficiently ... they tend to become chilled more easily in cold weather, and they have superior rhythmic abilities.

Even a national teachers' union in Britain has endorsed this final point by suggesting that black pupils have 'natural rhythm' which will enable them to gain some success in the artistic and sporting rather than the more cerebral areas of the school curriculum (Carrington, 1983).

The *psychological* argument is that blacks are better than whites at coping with stress, having a greater capacity to relax and stay 'physically loose' under competitive pressure. The third, *historical*, argument is what we might term the 'survival of the physically fittest' perspective. Afro-Caribbeans and North American blacks had to endure slavery in conditions which were so onerous that only the fittest survived. Therefore, factors such as power, speed and agility were disproportionately bred into the 'gene pool' of this racial group.

Cashmore's critique of Kane's quasi-scientific racism is ingenious, since he does not shrink from demonstrating how both black and white players/ athletes, coaches and administrators tacitly or overtly collude with some of these pervasive and persuasive views. Cashmore notes that data for race-linked physiological characteristics is drawn from only a limited sample of high-achieving athletes and, moreover, that no account is taken of the variation *within* the black sporting population – variations which are greater than *between* black and white. Kane's one-dimensional view is similarly criticized with reference to the psychological argument. Here, Cashmore notes that blacks are just as stressed as whites within sporting competition, but he notes how blacks both collude and use this image, and how whites might also get 'psyched out' by 'falling foul of their own myths'. Linked to this, Cashmore cites research which suggests that blacks are better at 'reactive' sports (e.g. athletics, games) than other sporting challenges, and that this is the primary reason for patterns of over- and under-representation! The historical argument is treated with disdain. How 'pure' is the black 'gene pool'? Are not qualities such as ingenuity, intelligence and tact just as important for survival under slavery as physical characteristics such as power, speed and agility?

A self-fulfilling prophecy: channelling blacks into sport

It is important now to address the consequences of this misguided logic. The logic is as follows: blacks have natural ability in sport; therefore it can do little harm to realize this potential by encouraging participation in sport. Over-representation and blacks' outstanding results confirm and reproduce the validity of the original belief.

Other than this ideology, there are many dimensions of racism which can be expressed institutionally in the form of systematic practices that, in effect, deny and exclude blacks from access to valued social resources (e.g. educational qualifications). It is this example of institutional racism which is addressed by

Leamon and Carrington (1985); that physical education in schools systematically 'reproduces ethnic
marginality' in society, by acting as a 'side-track'
away from academic skills. Cashmore (1982) makes
similar points in Chapter 6 of his book 'Black
Sportsmen'. Each of these provide an explanation of
the over-representation of Afro-Caribbean children in
school sport.

Leamon and Carrington argue that the over-representation of Afro-Caribbean pupils in school sport is
the outcome of 'channelling' by teachers, who tend to
view this group stereotypically as having skills of the
body rather than the mind. Channelling *towards*
sport results in channelling *away* from other aspects
of a school's curriculum. By encouraging these
'motor-minded' pupils into sport (perhaps at the
expense of their academic studies and by using sport
as a mechanism of social control) teachers inadver-
tently reinforce Afro-Caribbean academic failure. This
facilitates the reproduction of the black worker as
wage labour at the lower end of the employment scale.
Without anti-racist intervention, they will continue to
function as a repository of menial wage labour but
also as sporting 'gladiators' for white British society
(Cashmore, 1982). Note also, that for every successful
'gladiator' there are hundreds of frustrated and
disaffected young black people who, spurred on by
black role models in sport, find that sporting success,
fame and money are a very rare commodity (as it is for
white men and fewer women).

For both Leamon and Carrington, and for
Cashmore therefore, the over-representation of black
people in sports is evidence of institutional racism at
work, rather than evidence of equality of opportunity!

Life at the top: stacking the odds

The number of black players in British sports has
risen significantly over the past two decades, but
research both in Britain and the USA illustrates that

stereotypical images of the abilities of blacks (and whites) affects the allocation of playing positions within team games such as soccer, American football, and rugby (there are no data on women's sports). This differential allocation stems from discrimination on the basis of assumed mental and physical abilities. There are two related elements to this discrimination: (a) stacking, and (b) centrality/non-centrality of position.

Stacking refers to the over-representation of black and white players in specific positions within the team, and concomitantly an under-representation in other positions. **Centrality/non-centrality** refers to the levels of interaction with other team-mates, and the degree to which a player must coordinate tasks and activities with other team members. Central positions are deemed to demand qualities such as leadership, decision-making, intelligence, intra-team coordination; namely power and authority over playing strategy.

According to research in the USA in the late 1970s, the more central the position, the greater the likelihood that it will be held by a white rather than a black. The explanation for this is the assumption that black players lack the mental ability to play in key decision-making strategic roles but are strong and, above all, fast. A graphic illustration of this comes from Coakley's (1986) account of black/white playing positions in baseball and American football.

In American football, black players were over-represented in positions such as wide-receiver and linebacker, and under-represented in central positions such as quarterback. In baseball, 78% of infield (central) positions were occupied by whites, 22% by blacks, while 48% of outfield positions (non-central) were occupied by whites, 52% by blacks.

Other more recent research includes Lavoie's (1989) linkage of stacking with salary discrimination in US professional ice hockey, and Leonard's (1990) demonstration that major league baseball players are much more likely to be recruited into managerial positions if they occupy 'central' playing positions (see above). Hallinan (1991) demonstrates a positional segregation between aborigines and whites in Australian rugby league, and through analysing handling and tackling counts, shows that aborigines are over-represented in marginal playing positions. Stebbins (1993) ameliorates the dominant view that blacks only are stacked. He points to evidence of 'white stacking' in the Canadian leagues of American football. His explanation is that US (especially black) players are imported to strengthen teams and to occupy central positions in the various teams.

There is some evidence to suggest that stacking is not prevalent in all team games. Coakley (1986) calls American football a 'highly bureaucratised' sport, with much more strictly segregated roles than other team games. Edwards (1973) notes that the role responsibilities associated with basketball are not so clearly delineated. Likewise, soccer is a more fluid, freer game where team play is marked by an exceptionally high degree of interdependence, i.e. interaction between players in different positions occurs much more frequently. Therefore, it might be difficult to generalize the stacking/centrality argument across team games which are structured to allow different group dynamics.

British stacking

Maguire (1990), however, argues that this form of discrimination against blacks is also apparent in British soccer. Based upon a systematic analysis of the Football League in 1985–86, he notes a disproportionate representation of blacks in certain positions across all four divisions (Table 5.3).

This suggests that some form of stacking exists in soccer. Blacks are under-represented in goalkeeping and in midfield – a pattern which is even more marked when wide and central midfielders are disaggregated. Furthermore, and borrowing from

Table 5.3 Position occupancy among black Football League
players, 1985-86

Position	Percentage (n = 111)
Goalkeeper	0.9 (1)
Fullback	19.8 (22)
Centreback	12.6 (14)
Midfield	15.3 (17)
Forwards	51.3 (57)

Source: Maguire (1990), by permission

FIFA, Maguire assigns goalkeepers, centrebacks,
central midfield players and central strikers to the
central category, whereas fullbacks, wide/support
midfield players and wide/support forwards are
assigned to the non-central category (Table 5.4). On
this basis, he argues that racial segregation in British
soccer is linked to centrality.

Table 5.4 Race and centrality of position in the English
Football League

Position	White (%)	Black (%)	Total (100%)
Central	652 (95.5)	31 (4.5)	683
Non-central	682 (89.5)	80 (10.5)	762
Total	1334 (92.3)	111 (7.7)	1445

Source: Maguire (1990), by permission

Among black players, 28% occupy central positions
and 72% play in non-central positions. When white
players are considered, there is only a 2% difference
between occupancy of positions. Evidence is sparse
from other team games, but Wedderburn (1990)
points out that, in the 1986–87 season, seven of the
nine black players in First Division Rugby Union
clubs played on the wing. His thesis is called 'You're

black, you're fast, you're on the wing'! A survey of black players in the 1st and A teams of professional Rugby League teams was conducted in the period November 1989 to January 1990 (Wilkinson, 1990). In all, thirty-two of the players were from ethnic minorities, thirty of Afro-Caribbean origin, two of Asian origin. Of these, twenty-five played as wing three-quarters, and only two (Hanley of Wigan and Drummond of Warrington) were the captain of the team. Of the seven players who were not wings, five were in other non-central positions, of prop, or second-row.

Is there life after playing?

Who runs British sport? The answer is (usually male) whites, and there seems to be few opportunities and minimal representation of blacks in the governing, coaching and administration of sports. Not only are blacks over-represented in subordinate playing positions, but there is under-representation and marked power discrepancies in the organization of British sport. Blacks then tend to have a foreshortened career in sport, limited to playing. Is this an instance of institutionalized racism which results in the continuation of a privileged position of whites at the expense of blacks? Lashley (1991) suggests that the marginalization of blacks in positions of power and influence can be addressed, and notes that one of the areas identified by the Sports Council's review of British sport's organization and structure is:

> the problems and inadequacies relating to the identification, training, employment, and deployment of (black) coaches.

Anti-racist strategies should be high on this agenda, as a critical element of positive action. A similar issue is addressed with respect to women in a later chapter; namely the disproportionate power and influence of men in the control and bureaucracy of sport, both nationally and internationally.

South Asians and sport

Stereotyping

People of Asian descent are not as 'visible' in British sport as either whites or Afro-Caribbeans, and are under-represented in most sports with the possible exceptions of cricket, hockey and badminton. As with people of Afro-Caribbean descent, racism at individual and institutional levels is apparent in sports involvement by South Asians. At an individual level there is evidence that South Asians experience racist abuse in schools, in sports clubs, and even sports spectating (Williams, 1994). At an institutional level, Fleming (1990, 1994) reviews evidence of stereotypical assumptions about South Asians in schools as being 'academic but not interested in sport'.

Typically, Asians are seen as not interested in, or too frail for, contact sports, as lacking stamina and as being poorly coordinated. This is especially evident in perceptions of Asian girls who are, it is assumed, not socialized into sports-related play activities at an early age, who take on major domestic responsibilities in the home, and who are positively discouraged to take part in sports which conflict with gender-appropriate behaviour as culturally prescribed. An outcome of this negative stereotyping is that, just as Afro-Caribbeans are channelled *into* sport, South Asians are, effectively channelled *out of*, at least some, sports. In addition, assumptions about sporting preferences of Asians (e.g. do not like swimming or rugby, but do like cricket and badminton) results in what Fleming calls 'funnelling' into some sports and away from others in school PE curricula. The problem is exemplified by the sponsoring by professional football organizations of a report entitled 'Asians Can't Play Football'. The authors, the Asian Social Development Agency, expose the complex of factors which effectively funnel South Asians away from soccer.

From ethnographic data, Fleming (1994) also points out that this pernicious stereotypical thinking, reinforced by the absence of sporting role models, is reproduced by South Asians who become victims of their own myths. He writes:

> When stereotypes become embedded in the dominant culture, they are often internalised by the very people to whom the stereotypes apply.

Heterogeneity

The first step in challenging stereotypical characterizations of South Asians and sport is to recognize the diversity of people collectively labelled as 'South Asian'. This appellation masks differences in terms of language, culture, religion, social mobility, attitudes towards gender-roles and, most obviously, of nationality; namely Indian, Pakistani, Bangladeshi and East African (primarily Kenyan) Asians. This diversity is recognized in a recent Sports Council project, reported by Carroll (1993), which aimed to explore the relationship between ethnicity, culture and participation in sport. The groups studied were African, Bangladeshi, Caribbean, Chinese, East Africa Asian, Indian, Pakistani and a comparable white group in the Greater Manchester area. Some of the findings were:

- nearly 50% of Bangladeshi, African and Pakistani, and over a third of Indian females, did no sport or physical recreation at all
- the Chinese and the white British are the most active, and the Pakistani and Bangladeshi the least active in sport
- for most groups, females accepted domestic responsibilities as central to their lives in ways men did not, thereby limiting the amount of perceived free time
- the male/female difference in participation is greater for Muslims, Hindus and Sikhs than it is for Christians and non-believers

- there is an inter-ethnic difference in sport prefer-ence, but overall major team games and outdoor pursuits lack popularity (with the exception of basketball for Afro-Caribbeans and cricket for the three South Asian groups)
- ninety per cent of all friendships (in sports groups or otherwise) are between people from the same ethnic group
- ethnicity, religion and gender combine to affect sports participation significantly.

Much of this is confirmed and elaborated upon by Fleming (1994), who identifies the following ethno-cultural factors as being critical for an understanding of South Asians and sports participation:

- religion, and sects within a religion
- class, mobility and caste
- family (structure, size and relationships)
- place of origin (nationality, region, urban/rural)
- immigration (place, timing, causes)
- linguistic group
- generation (and degree of acculturation)
- gender and kinship networks.

Fleming's earlier ethnographic study (1990) revealed different attitudes towards physical educa-tion and sport by young South Asians in North London. All sociological studies of youth culture reveal significant if subtle lines of fracture, which give rise to different identities and status, and this study explores the social dynamics between four discernible groups of Asian young people; namely 'Straights', 'Boffins', 'Victims' and 'Street Kids'. These informal and shifting groups are distinguished in terms of their attitude to education, the occupational status of parents or social class, whether they are first-, second-, or even third-generation British, and their attitudes to and evaluation of school sport and phys-ical education. According to Fleming, the four most important influences upon sports participation are ethnicity (which includes religion and place of origin), class, gender and generation.

Colonizing, separation, and resistance

Carroll (1993) indicated that most friendships in his research population were between people from the same ethnic group. This is borne out in sports teams representing localized community groups and by the patterns of usage of local sport and leisure centres. In Bradford's Manningham community recreation centre, for instance, the uptake of activities and the scheduling of use is contoured by ethnic divisions, reproducing the social networks and spatial and cultural segregation of the local area. In some cases, however, **separation** is a deliberate strategy in order to retain control over sport. In other cases, it is an emergent consequence of the 'ghettoization', particularly of inner-city communities, and of the social dynamics between the ethnic groups.

An extreme example of colonizing and separation in the face of institutionalized racism is all-Asian cricket leagues in Yorkshire, as documented, in 1991, in the BBC's 'The Race Game'. At this time, no British South Asian had played cricket for Yorkshire, and very few young Asian players had been invited to join the county's youth development scheme, the Cricket Academy. Yet thousands were playing in competitive leagues, particularly in the Bradford and Sheffield areas. It seemed that youth development strategies and the locus of power within the county's game completely neglected a major constituency of potential players. The outcome, throughout the 1980s, was little short of apartheid – separate and unequal development according to ethnicity.

As with any discriminatory practices which perpetuate social inequalities, critique needs to be followed by the formulation of policy and initiatives designed to alleviate social inequality such as:

- equalizing opportunity and access to sport participation, coaching, administration
- combating stereotypical thinking about black and South Asian people among coaches and administrators
- exploring the sports needs of all black and South Asian people, men and women, young and old
- marketing sport among black and South Asian organizations/communities.

Sports policy

Although the voluntary sector of sports provision has barely started to address these issues, in the public sector of sports provision, policy articulates around two broad strategies which can be called: (a) liberal multiculturalism, and (b) anti-racism.

A **liberal** approach aims to challenge stereotypical thinking, raise consciousness through race-awareness training, remove discrimination and try to equalize access to sport, and provide opportunities for different cultural groups to pursue their own cultural forms (e.g. Asian dance/theatre, Kabbadi, arm-wrestling, Koh and Layzeem).

A more radical approach which we might term **anti-racism** is based on the premise that this liberal strategy does not challenge institutionalized racism, and ignores the continuation of a white power-structure in sport which must be challenged. A critique of the organization of sport is achieved by situating it within capitalism, patriarchy and white colonialism. Anti-racist strategies include **separation**, **resistance** and **positive action**, in order to equalize power between different ethnic groups. Typically, however, public sector strategies are primarily characterized by liberal multiculturalism.

However, the Regional Council for Sport and Recreation in the West Midlands, an area with a high proportion of people from ethnic minorities, combine elements of both strategies in their Policy Statement

(December 1990) on Sport, Race and Racism. The following summarizes the main elements of this statement, and also provides a summary of the key issues addressed in this chapter. It provides some lessons for sports practitioners who want to address racism in sport.

Lessons for practice

1 Racism in sport is fundamentally about **power** in sport, e.g. decision-making, allocation of resources, the control and appointment of staff.
2 The participation of black people in sport is often considered not to be an issue because of the high visibility of black people. However, this high-visibility model gives a false picture of black participation.
3 Black participation in sport – by age, sex or ethnic groups – can and is limited by **stereotyping**, lack of access, lack of finances. Governing bodies require race-awareness training and to be confronted with the many sporting stereotypes they may have of black/Asian sportspeople.
4 An ageist view of black participation is given. The needs of black people are much wider than just the needs and rights of young people.
5 Black sportspersons to their detriment may be encouraged into competitive and professional sports to seek to make a living, rather than viewing sport as a leisure pursuit.
6 Sporting opportunity is limited to a few easily accessible sports; access to other sports needs to be developed.
7 Sporting opportunity is limited to playing. There are very few black senior administrators or coaches in sport in this country. This situation must be changed.
8 An **ethnicized** view of sport exists, with an exclusive focus on Afro-Caribbean participation. Other ethnic groups needs have not been fully explored, particularly South Asian.

9 Sport is often provided through the state as a means of social control rather than for personal and community development.

Sport, ability and disability

Introduction

An impairment – whether sensory, mental or physical – restricts an individual in executing some skills, performing tasks or participating in certain activities or movements. It is estimated that six million of the British population have some form of impairment, including paraplegics, blind and partially-sighted, people with cerebral palsy, deaf and/or dumb people, autistic people, those who have survived polio, diabetes, multiple sclerosis or a birth defect. This translates into a range of different sensory, physical or mental problems; 5% are wheelchair users, 55% have mental impairment, 20% have sensory impairment, and 20% are ambulatory but with physical impairment.

Some are born with impairments, for others it is acquired at varying points in one's life; for some, the condition is only temporary, for others it is permanent. It is estimated that over 70% of the population will suffer a temporary disabling condition in the course of their lives. This is a large and heterogeneous group of people, the differences within which are as significant as the condition of impairment.

Society disables

In the introduction, the term **impairment** was used rather than **disability**. The distinction is crucial, since impairment refers to a medical condition, whereas disability connotes both the physical and social disadvantages experienced by a large group of people, in sport and elsewhere. The term **disablism** therefore suggests that medical divisions become crystallized into social divisions and, consequently, inequities in the **ability** of people to participate fully as members of the community; hence the title of this chapter.

This reasoning is based upon an understanding of two competing perspectives about disability. The traditional **medical** perspective sees disability as the loss or reduction of functional ability and activity that is consequent upon impairment. The main implications of this functional definition are that the disabled person must be **helped** and a large army of professionals (therapists, social workers, doctors, specialist teachers and carers) has developed around the management of disabled people. Instead of the physical and social world being adapted for *all* people, disabled people have their own services, separated out from the rest of social life. The image of disabled people in this essentially therapeutic perspective is primarily one of dependence and passivity, rather than independence and self-advocacy.

In recognition of the limitations of the medical perspective, a **social** perspective has been developed which involves a radical shift away from individual problems of impairment, towards a recognition of how inadequately designed environments, social organizations, attitudes and assumptions, impose limitations on disabled people. It is **society which discriminates, handicaps, and imposes barriers on disabled people**. It is social organizations, developed with the needs and conveniences of non-disabled people in mind, which must change. This more politicized perspective seeks to maximize the extent to which an historically disempowered group of people are able to realize their social and political rights to full citizenship.

In line with this second approach to disability, the Minister of Sport's Review Group into sport for people with disabilities published 'Building on Ability' (HMSO, 1989). This report contained a number of recommendations for sports organizations in the public and voluntary sectors centring on the need to 'refocus sport for people with disabilities away from disability' (Marshall, 1991). The title of the report is instructive, since it is based on a concern that stereotypes must be diminished by considering all people in terms of their abilities, not disabilities, and not on the basis of myths, fears or ignorance, i.e. disablist practice. The list below provides a summary of some of the main recommendations of the report:

- National governing bodies of sport to recognize their responsibility for disabled people, to include disability issues in coach training programmes, to ensure representation in the governance of the sport by disabled people and disability sports organizations, if necessary, to extend or rewrite rules to include versions for people with disabilities, and where appropriate to integrate disabled into mainstream sport.
- Local authorities to assume responsibility for ensuring provision at local level, to consult disabled people in the construction of facilities, and to ensure that compulsory competitive tendering does not disadvantage these people.
- To reorganize disability sports associations (which had been principally constructed around medical definitions of disability) to ensure greater co-ordination and development of sporting opportunity.
- The media to promote positive images of disabled sportsmen and women as opposed to images which reinforce passivity and dependence.

The 'Building on Ability' report only provides recommendations, rather than statutory requirements. However, these were taken up in 1993 by the Sports Council, which has provided guidelines for sports governing bodies, and by the British Sports Association for the Disabled (BSAD). The formation of the Federation of Disability Sports Organisations in Yorkshire and Humberside provides an example of greater liaison between disability sports organizations, by incorporating British Blind Sports, the British Deaf Sports Council, Disport, and the UK Sports Association for people with a Mental Handicap. Arguably, however, the underlying problem of disablism remains, as Borrett *et al.* (1995) state:

> Discourse ... still tends to be dominated by professional non-disabled people that perpetuates a world of sport based on non-disabled norms.

However, at the level of national mainstream and disability sports organizations there is a discernible shift towards more **inclusive** and away from **exclusive** and segregated provision. Critical in this regard is the necessity for adequate resourcing; in terms of the training of sports teachers, coaches and organizers, and also specialist facility and equipment provision. The recent emphasis on inclusive provision leads to a consideration of the constraints which disabled people experience with respect to participation in sport.

The accessibility of sports

Full participation in sporting communities is ensured only when there is equitable access and opportunity. To overcome inequitable access and opportunity, the following need to be addressed:

- perceptual barriers
- attitudinal barriers
- physical barriers
- financial barriers
- adapting and modifying sports
- school physical education.

Perceptual barriers

This refers to disabled people's awareness of the existence of facilities for sport, and of the organizations which specifically cater for the needs of disabled people. Many have little contact with disability sports organizations, little or no knowledge of the opportunities so afforded, or that mainstream sports organizations are assuming an increased role in sports provision for disabled people.

Most significantly, however, many disabled people have had little previous opportunity, at critical learning periods in childhood, to develop the basic movement abilities upon which more specific sports skills are based. Lack of previous experience in sport often translates into a low assessment of one's own capabilities, and consequently avoidance of sports challenges through fear of failure or ridicule.

Also, mainstream sports providers, organizers and coaches, having had little opportunity to work with disabled people, are unlikely to have a full understanding of the specific challenges facing disabled people.

Attitudinal barriers

As with race and gender, disability awareness training is about changing attitudes and confronting myths and misconceptions about disability which stem from a lack of understanding. Insidious labelling of groups (e.g. *the* disabled, *the* handicapped, *the* blind) creates crude distinctions which forefronts the medical condition, minimizes individual differences and underplays abilities. The Scottish Sports Council, in 1994, discussed attitudinal barriers thus (but note the assumption that the readership is able-bodied):

> In the case of a person who is disabled, the more visible and obvious the disability the more likely it is that the disability will become the main focus of attention. We will then use

this visual information to determine in our own minds, the capabilities of that person. Such assessments are rarely accurate and often result in the disabled person feeling patronised, inadequate and dependent. On the other hand, when we perceive and expect a person who is disabled to be resourceful, with a potential for a full and rewarding life, independence and life can be enhanced.

Physical barriers

This is the most obvious connotation of 'accessibility'. The Disabled Persons Act 1981 made it a statutory obligation for the design of local authorities' sports facilities to conform to minimum access requirements. But this was not retrospective and did not include buildings built before that date. Haywood *et al.* (1995) list some of the extensive measures that need to be considered:

> toilet and changing facilities, ramps, lifts, wide car-parking bays, hand rails on stair flights, lever taps on wash basins, automatic doors, non-slip floors, signs in braille, signs in a colour appropriate for partially-sighted, accessible bar counters, lift control buttons, vending machines.

Minimum access requirements is not the same as access on equal terms with able-bodied people and this is seldom achieved. In practice, the ideal of equal access is balanced with the realism of cost-benefits (e.g. a lift to enable access to a water slide). Sargent (1987) advocates that concerns about cost should be outweighed by concerns with equity, but public sector spending constraints are likely to ensure continued inequality of access.

Financial barriers

There is an economic gap between disabled people and their able-bodied peers, which means that disabled people do not have the same disposable income to spend on sport and other leisure activity. In 1988, only 31% of disabled people of working age were in employment. Also, those in employment earned, on average, only 80% of the salaries of able-bodied peers. Three-quarters of disabled adults have to rely on state benefits as their main source of income (Hunt, 1993) and finally, the incomes of non-pensioner disabled families are only 72% of the national average (HMSO, 1989). Whatever statistical measure is taken, disabled people are financially disadvantaged, thereby compounding the barriers to participation identified earlier.

These four barriers to participation feature in Henderson's (1995) insightful analysis of how women with physical disabilities negotiate with constraints on leisure activity. Three groups are identified: passive responders, achievers and attempters, who vary in their ability and motivation to negotiate constraints successfully. Typical constraints include:

- energy deficiency
- time shrinkage (because of the demands of the disability)
- lack of opportunities and choices (had to be concerned with attitudinal and physical accessibility of certain leisure activities, e.g. special reservations)
- dependency on others
- concerns for physical and psychological safety.

Adapting and modifying sports

Games and sports provide gratuitously difficult challenges which sustain their interest and appeal for participants precisely because of these characteristics. For disabled people, the challenges are even greater because of functional impairment.

Functional rather than medical definitions of disability are more useful with respect to sports involvement. Brown (1987) identifies six problems which might interfere with perceptual-motor performance in sports:

- lack of previous experience from being overprotected and sheltered and missing critical early learning
- hand and arm impairment (strength and control)
- ability to move with freedom (restriction of walking with assistive devices, wheelchairs)
- lack of voluntary control due to cerebral dysfunction
- sensory impairment (visual, auditory, kinaesthetic)
- psychological learning difficulties (visual-motor, visual-perceptual, spatial disorders).

Although there are occasions when some disabled people can compete on equal terms with able-bodied peers (e.g. archery), in many cases the selection, modification and adaptation of sporting activities is necessary to make them accessible. Satisfaction only comes from positive experiences and total involvement, and this can only happen if the abilities and skills of the performer are commensurate with the modified or adapted challenge. For example, the British Sports Association for the Disabled provide the following checklist of ways which individual and team games might be adapted to make them accessible to disabled people:

- use larger/smaller balls
- lighter equipment, e.g. beach balls, volleyballs
- lower net height
- shorter handled racquets/sticks
- brighter coloured equipment
- tactile/touch reference points
- callers or a sound source for direction control
- malleable equipment for those with poor grip, e.g. bean bags
- foam equipment to limit bounce heights
- limiting the area of play
- increasing the number on each team
- allowing ambulant participants to push wheelchair users

- give players specific areas so that all can play without being intimidated by more able players
- using DIY equipment to facilitate participation, e.g. pieces of guttering for bowling, blocks of wood for resting snooker cues on, batting tees to support a ball before hitting.

All such modifications are based upon an assessment of the abilities of the **performer**, together with analysis of the psychomotor requirements of the sporting **task**. If there is a congruence between these two elements, then accessibility is assured.

In response to 'Building on Ability', and drawing upon the expertise of well-established disability sports organizations, many governing bodies have developed policies and programmes covering coach education and training of officials, the technical adaptation of equipment and rules, establishing links with clubs and developing award schemes. The British Canoe Union is cited as an example of good practice by the Sports Council (1993) in this respect.

School physical education

The Education Act 1988 stipulated that many disabled young people should be integrated into mainstream schools, and the subsequent development of a National Curriculum included a commitment that children with 'special educational needs' should have access to the same curriculum as other children and that curriculum delivery should change in order for this to happen. Arguably, the successful integration of disabled children into most aspects of the curriculum has been achieved, but physical education and sport impose specific demands.

Physical education provides a crucial opportunity for young people to develop a range of movement experiences in individual and team games, swimming, dance, gymnastics and outdoor pursuits.

Jowsey (1992) argues, however, that few disabled people can follow a school PE curriculum without adaptation, and that a flexible, creative approach to curriculum content by empathic PE teachers is required. A study by Borrett *et al.* (1995) concluded that 'many young disabled people do not receive a range of movement experiences appropriate to their abilities in mainstream schools'. More specifically:

- physical education is sometimes regarded as a peripheral curriculum area from which pupils can be withdrawn for physiotherapy or remedial academic work
- with respect to PE, the problem is compounded by disabled young people being dispersed so that they are a small minority in each school
- physical education staff have received little in-service training for disability, but there is some, if not extensive, evidence of modifying the curriculum to take account of special needs
- greater emphasis needs to be given to (a) the psycho- and perceptual-motor abilities of disabled young people, and (b) the differences between sports with respect to the skills and abilities demanded in meeting the challenge of the activity
- very few resources are available to adapt or modify sports in order to make them accessible
- few links have been established between schools and disability sports organizations; also, the involvement of young people with these organizations was either sporadic or non-existent.

There is clearly much to be done by both sports and education providers to meet the needs and rights of disabled people, and there needs to be a distinction between PE for therapy reasons and PE for PE's sake! This study also stressed that, as with the non-disabled population, the material and cultural resources of parents (expressed in time, disposable income, leisure interests and expertise) are critical for opening up opportunities for young disabled people, especially when mobility is a problem.

Integration

Integration is but one element of broader debates about the extent to which disabled people are able to realize their social and political rights to full citizenship. The issue of integration is a key aspect of both the government's 'Building on Ability' report and of the Education Reform Act 1988. Governing bodies for sport are recommended, and mainstream schools are required, to cater equitably for the needs of disabled people. According to Marshall (1983), the three main barriers to integration are attitudinal, architectural and administrative, the first of which is probably the most important. He argues that

> attitudes about disablement ... have been crucially important in determining the social context within which disabled people participate in sport, and have helped to establish an administrative structure which may in itself reinforce segregation.

In recognition of this, governing bodies and disability sports organizations have developed inclusive strategies to enhance the sporting opportunities for disabled people. With respect to sports organizations, integration has a number of connotations:

- ensuring adequate representation in decision-making processes in governing bodies
- training programmes for officials (referees, coaches) to ensure that disabled people have equal access to professional expertise
- organizing competitive sports for disabled athletes in conjunction with able-bodied athletes, thereby raising the profile of the former
- fully integrated sport when (certain) disabilities are irrelevant.

The first two of these are largely a matter of organization and resourcing. The third, however, has spawned
considerable debate. The Amateur Swimming
Association, for example, has recently incorporated
events for disabled people within their Olympic trials
programme, and most people are aware of the wheelchair marathon competitions alongside high-profile
events such as the London and Boston marathons.
There are also moves to incorporate disabled events
into the Olympic Games, although at present the
Paralympics remain just that – a *parallel* set of events
which receives minuscule publicity in comparison to
the traditional event.

Marshall (1983) points out that active sports participation spans elite competitive sport and grass-roots
recreational sport, and in either case we can usefully
distinguish between segregated, parallel and fully
integrated activities. The feasibility of integrated or
parallel competitive sport will vary according to the
nature and severity of the disability, but there are
fewer restrictions with respect to recreational sport.

Competitive sport

Equity issues go beyond the grass-roots levels of
involvement (**foundation** and **participation** levels in
Sport's Council terminology) to encompass elite levels
of **performance** and **excellence**. Marshall (1991)
stresses that disabled sportspeople are first and fore-
most canoeists, athletes, basketball players, skiers
not paraplegics, blind, amputees, etc., and should be
treated as such; as different sports competitors but
deserving equitable treatment.

The refocus away from disability and towards sport
is evident in the formation of the International
Paralympic Committee in 1989, organized through
national affiliation and sports-specific federations
rather than through medical diagnostic categories of
disability. Competitive programmes are facilitated by

the Profile System developed by Meaden (1992), the aim of which is to group competitors with particular functional abilities within each sport. There are thirty-nine profiles altogether, which include thirty for those with locomotor impairments, three for those with sensory impairment, three for those with learning difficulties, one for other disabilities, and one for non-disabled people (Figure 6.1).

Since it includes all disabilities regardless of the medical definition, the system ensures that an athlete will be competing against people with similar levels of functional ability. Cooperation between medical personnel, sports experts and disabled people enables profiles to be grouped together in a sports-specific way, to create conditions of equality which is the basis for meaningful competitive sport.

Table 6.1 illustrates how this works in practice with reference to table tennis, a sport which has a large participant base organized into eight competitive groups.

Table 6.1 The Profile System: table tennis

Group	Profiles	Description
1	1–5	Wheelchair competitors with poor arm function
2	6, 7, 9	Wheelchair competitors with poor arm function and/or balance dysfunction
3	8, 10, 11	Wheelchair competitors
4	12–14, 21	Ambulatory with poor arm function
5	17, 18, 20, 22, 25, 27, 29	Ambulatory with poor arm function and/or balance dysfunction
6	15, 16, 19, 23, 24, 26, 28, 30	Ambulatory
7	38	Sensory dysfunction
8	39–41	Cerebral dysfunction

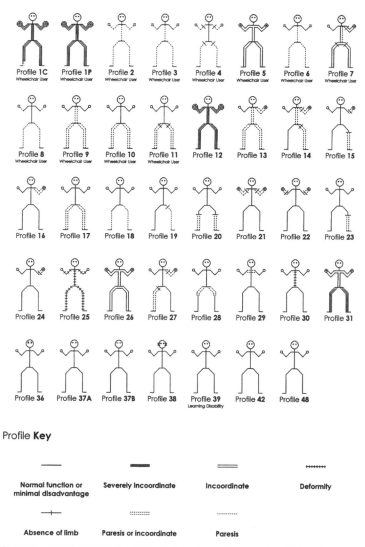

Figure 6.1 The profile system
(*Source*: British Sports Association for the Disabled, October 1996, by permission)

Different but equitable?

Most current developments in disabled sport aim to provide equitable access to sports opportunity and physical education, to de-institutionalize members of our society previously segregated in special schools and in segregated sports provision, and to challenge perceptual barriers about disability founded upon prejudice and ignorance. These eventuate in issues about equality but also about equity.

Equality, meaning sameness, directs attention to access to resources, to trained sports personnel, to specialist facilities, to support participation at both grass roots and elite levels. Equity, meaning justice and fairness, brings into sharp relief issues about segregated, parallel and integrated provision. At a surface level, and as has been noted earlier, this involves governing bodies assuming an increased responsibility for provision across the whole of the ability range. Traditionally, governing bodies have managed sports competitions in a hierarchical fashion according to ability. Their most recent task is merely to extend that provision to a further range of abilities. Just as one's local soccer team is unlikely ever to play a Premier League club, so it is often inappropriate for disabled athletes to compete directly with non-disabled people, where the disability is a critical factor.

Moreover, some would argue that the whole value-structure of performance-sport has to be questioned; to think about sporting achievement in non-quantitative ways, as not necessarily being evaluated in terms of objective performance levels, but rather to re-vision sports participation to emphasize qualitative aspects of experience in sports environments. The exclusionary emphasis on winning in so much modern sport, in which all those who do not win are understood as losers, is as inappropriate for many disabled people as it is for much of the rest of the population.

Consequently, the key issue for disabled people –

and for others – is not to mimic the non-disabled in sport, but rather to celebrate difference, acknowledge abilities in modified sports, and to recognize, on the basis of those abilities, outstanding sporting achievements. The overarching issue is to win control over the conditions and circumstances of one's life, and it should be for disabled people to choose whether integrated, parallel or segregated provision is most appropriate in that regard.

Sport and gender

Gender issues in sport are not synonymous with women's issues in sport. However, it is principally feminist scholarship which has developed critiques of the practice and organization of modern sports, the values which are celebrated, and the complex ways in which sport reproduces gender inequity, with women being in a disadvantageous position. This chapter therefore is primarily, if not exclusively, about women in sport; but is there a social problem?

What's the problem?

Sporting opportunity and participation by women in sport has increased considerably over the past twenty years. This is borne out by statistical information about indoor and outdoor sports published by the Sports Council (1988, 1994) and by membership profiles of a range of national sports organizations. Indeed, a credible argument might be mounted that sport is relatively accessible to women, that there are not any marked discriminatory practices, and consequently that the position of women in sport is not a social problem! Support for this view might include the following:

- There have been massive advances towards political equality and legal rights, culminating in the Equal Opportunities Act 1970 and the Sex Discrimination Act 1975.
- Women's lives are not so privatized and constrained as they were in the past.

- Attitudes about what is socially acceptable in terms of masculine/feminine behaviour have liberalized.
- Technological advances have removed the drudgery from domestic labour; birth-control has empowered women with small planned families as the norm.
- More women are in paid work and financially independent than ever before; more families have moved towards a 'symmetrical' relationship (Young and Wilmott, 1973) between partners, characterized by shared decision-making, joint control over finances, shared domestic chores. In short, women now experience far less constraints on their leisure time.
- Sport is now fashionable and 'chic', thereby loosening perceptual barriers to participation. Sport does not necessarily compromise self-image, nor dominant images of femininity.
- According to the Sports Council, participation by women in indoor sport has increased approximately threefold in the last decade, and by twofold in outdoor sport (although this masks regional and class differences). The General Household Survey shows that between 1977 and 1987 the percentage of female participants increased in all sports activity groups except those taking part in outdoor sport only.

Women are not a homogeneous group. They comprise 52% of the population, and the contrasts *between* men and women are not as great as differences *among* either women or men according to their ethnic identity, marital status, social class, age and stage of the lifecycle. Therefore, any assertions about inequality or inequity on the basis merely of sex are both inaccurate and too generalized. Conscious of the main constituency of academe from which most feminist scholarship about sport flows, Dewar (1993) indicates the dangers of falsely universalizing white, middle class women's experiences, as being representative of all women's experience. She suggests that research and social policy must reflect the diverse ways in which the culture of sport create, support or even challenge disadvantage in all women's lives.

Nevertheless, many women feel that, in terms of sport, they are not discriminated against, that they have rich and varied sporting lifestyles, and do not experience constraints qualitatively different from men. However, despite this perception by some women, inequity remains, the basis of which is that there are identifiable patterns of domination and subordination according to gender, and that this has far-reaching consequences for sports and other institutional practices.

The total number of female participants in sport overall is half that of males, which in turn means that the possibilities of women reaching high levels of achievement are correspondingly reduced. Not only do fewer women than men play sport, but women play less often, and across a narrower range of sports (Clarke and Critcher, 1985). Social class, age, education, marriage and children all have more marked effects on women's participation than on men's. Responsibilities for child care, shortage of free time, lack of personal transport and money, and lower levels of self-confidence, are all reasons postulated for women having less opportunity than men to pursue sporting interests.

Sex, gender and sexism

Sex is assigned at birth and is understood as an ascribed biological characteristic. **Gender** has nothing to do with biology, but rather refers to all the differences between men and women which derive from social expectations about appropriate behaviour, interests, abilities and attitudes for masculine and feminine identity. Whereas sex is ascribed, gender is achieved, mostly tacitly, through socialization experiences. When gender relations, within sport or elsewhere, subordinate the interests of one sex to those of the other, inequity occurs. Moreover, whenever one group in society is dominant over others, there is invariably a set of beliefs, attitudes and sedimented practices which seek to legitimate the status quo, i.e. the existing set of inequalities. **Sexism**, therefore, refers to the ideology and the practices which justify and perpetuate an inequality between men and women, just as ideologies of racism, ageism and disablism sustain inequality on the basis of other facets of biology.

Critical sociologists argue that this **sexist** ideology pervades our whole culture, sustained by institutions in society including the family, the school (and the physical education curriculum), business (and the sport and leisure industry), government (and the management of both public and private leisure services), the media (and the sporting press and television).

Most writers about sexism in sport argue that the concept **sex-role** is unhelpful in addressing the relations between men and women. Sex-role refers to the social expectations considered appropriate for how males and females should behave – social and cultural constructions of masculine and feminine behaviour. Hall (1990) maintains that the term 'sex-role' suggests an unchanging, natural set of relationships between men and women, therefore failing to recognize that the 'masculine' and 'feminine' genders are socially constructed, historically specific and mediated by social class, race and ethnicity. The continued use of 'sex-role' in research, Hall maintains, hinders efforts to critique those very ideologies and practices which maintain the stereotypes in the first place.

Gender relations

Participation in sport by both men and women is contoured by gender relations, by conventional ideas about masculinity and femininity, by socially constructed images of the body, and by the networks of power and control in sports organizations. A statement such as this suggests that sport is essentially a conservative institution which both celebrates and sustains attitudes and practices inherited from the past. Conversely, however, sport might also be a place for challenging these time-worn and inequitable practices.

This is certainly the approach adopted by Hargreaves (1995). Drawing on a wide and eclectic range of research findings, Hargreaves provides a comprehensive review and analysis of socialization both into and out of (some) sports, the constraints women experience in sport, the highly selective and sexist nature of the media's portrayal of women's sport, and the relative lack of representation of women in positions of power in sports organizations.[1] Although highly critical of the diverse and subtle ways in which the practice and organization of sport reproduces gender inequities, Hargreaves indicates a growing acknowledgement of these inequities in Britain and of strategies to redress them; since critiques of male-dominated sports, to have any effect, must lead to action.

Research about women in sport reviewed by Hargreaves includes, first, the identification of gendered socialization practices with respect to sports and, secondly, a critique of male-dominated sports provision. This might be summarized as follows:

1 Analysis of **socialization** practices which effectively either channel girls out of sport altogether, or into sports which do not conflict with dominant images of femininity, namely:

[1] Jennifer Hargreaves (1995) has provided the most comprehensive and detailed analysis of gender issues in British sport and physical education. I am indebted to her for allowing me to review, however briefly, some of the main elements of her account; but the reader is advised to go to the original for a thorough understanding of sport and gender.

- child-rearing practices
- comics and magazines for children and adolescents
- teenage culture
- physical education in schools.

2 Analysis of British sporting **culture** and of sports **organizations** to illustrate either the marginalization or exploitation of women's practice, namely:

- the values and practices of the sports media
- male control of sports organizations
- the commercialization of the female body in sports
- under-resourcing of women's elite sport.

Socialization

Socialization refers to the processes whereby individuals learn to conform to social norms as culturally prescribed. Throughout childhood, this process of internalizing socially expected ways of behaving is largely unconscious and therefore experienced as natural, as taken-for-granted. Any attempt, therefore, to change people's commonsense assumptions about socially appropriate behaviour is problematic. Tacit or unacknowledged socialization into sport and physical recreation, or into all other aspects of popular culture, exerts a powerful influence upon us all.

Conscious of gender stereotyping, many parents try to treat their sons and daughters equally, provide similar play experiences, toys, books and movement experiences. Nevertheless, there is plenty of evidence to show that in general boys are encouraged into more adventurous activities, played with more roughly, allowed more freedom to explore their environment, display from an early age different motor abilities, and are given different toys and other playthings. Through their parents and the social networks to which they belong, through television programmes, advertisements, books, peer relationships and other aspects of daily life, children are constantly exposed to gendered behaviour and learn from those experiences. For example, Hargreaves cites Young's (1990) survey of children's textbooks which show that readers are thirteen times more likely to see images of an active man than an active woman. Children's magazines and comics treat sport differently for girls and boys, tending to portray sport as an integral and everyday activity for boys, yet an infrequent and marginal activity for girls. Moreover, where sports do feature, they are likely to be gender-appropriate; horse-riding, tennis, and swimming for girls, football (mainly) and other 'manly' sports for boys.

As every parent will know, early childhood influences of family and school are overlaid by teenage culture during adolescence. Adolescent culture for girls has little place for sport and, in contrast to boys, little peer group status is attached to sporting prowess. There is, however, a class dimension to this, since middle class girls are much more likely to value sports participation than working class girls, and to join clubs and organizations for other active leisure activities. In independent girls' schools there remains some social cachet from sporting ability. Nevertheless, preoccupations with fashion, music, clothes, romance and relationships are central to what Hargreaves calls 'the cult of adolescent femininity'. Unsurprisingly, this cult is reproduced in teenage magazines such as 'More' and 'Just Seventeen'. If sport and active recreation features at all, it tends to have an instrumental justification in terms of body care, looking good, being sexy ... a task which makes aerobics (and its derivatives) particularly attractive; certainly much more so than team sports like hockey and netball, which carry too many connotations of school, collective discipline and compulsion.

Formal schooling is arguably one of the most effective sites for challenging stereotypical views about gender-appropriate physical activity, and the recent introduction of a National Curriculum has provided an opportunity for physical educationalists to propose curricula common to both sexes. Hargreaves cites recommendations from the 'Final Report of the Physical Education Working Group' (HMSO, 1991) that all children should receive the same curriculum to avoid:

> future undesirable sex stereotyping activities ... a broad and balanced programme of physical education ... can help to extend boys' restricted perceptions of masculinity and masculine behaviour.

Such sentiments must be set into context. Traditionally, girls' and boys' secondary school physical education has been separate, while teacher training courses for men (e.g. Loughborough, Carnegie) and women (e.g. Chelsea, Bedford) drew upon different philosophies and traditions in physical education. Historically, there has always been a much greater emphasis upon creativity, the expressive, and aesthetic elements of movement experience in women's physical education courses, compared with adherence to fitness and competitive-oriented curricula in men's.

More recently, the advent of 'leisure education', the introduction of outdoor pursuits into PE curricula, and initiatives such as 'new image' rugby provide more opportunities for mixed-sex PE. Also, soccer is becoming one of the more popular team games for girls in schools. Nevertheless, Flintoff (1990) testifies to the persistence of separate and different (i.e. sexist) curricula for boys and girls, which do little to challenge gender inequity. For Scraton (1992), the issue is less about mixed PE, but rather about giving young women positive experiences which do not conflict with the adolescent culture of femininity. From an ethnographic study of Liverpool schools, Scraton found that girls' resistance to PE is based upon what they perceive to be on offer; namely the development of muscle, sweat, communal showering and changing facilities, childish asexual PE kit, and low-status activities. In contrast, Scraton suggests, women's PE needs to develop a new programme geared to assertiveness, confidence, health, fitness, and the capacity to challenge patriarchal definitions of submissiveness, passivity and dependence.

Culture and organization

The media

As noted in Chapter 3, sport is becoming increasingly dependent on the media. This, and the articulation of gendered values through television and the sports press, means, as Rowe and Brown (1994) argue, 'that any attempt to promote gender equity must of necessity emphasize the sphere of the media'. Women's sport is under-represented, being seldom more than 5% of the total coverage of sport in the national press. Men's sports dominate TV, with women's sports only receiving equal coverage during events such as Wimbledon and the Olympics. Otherwise, men's soccer, rugby, motor-racing, snooker, golf, horse-racing and cricket provide the staple diet of terrestrial TV. Satellite TV similarly shows a gender bias. The press also treats women differently to men, making references to sportswomen's marital status, their family and private lives, and providing sexualized images in photographs. For girls, the few role-models are limited mainly to feminine-appropriate sports such as tennis. Unsurprisingly, most of the media professionals who influence the content, style and nature of media-sport are men.

In response to a complaint to *The Guardian* newspaper about the neglect of women's sport in the press, Croft (1993) replied:

> Of course we are only interested in how well the shorts fit and whether the players have shaved their legs. After all, if you must insist in enforcing these quaint ideas that women can actually play competitive sport, let alone do it skilfully, on to our hallowed sports pages what kind of coverage do you expect? We men graciously donate most of the paper to girlie issues already, why must you muscle in on our little bit?

> Do you not realise what good chaps we all are? When we do mention you it is always prefaced by Women's (Sport) – everybody knows all sports coverage is all about men. And you do get a whole 5% of all sports coverage in the entire media all to yourselves to show how importantly you are perceived. Come on. You'll be expecting us to consider you as human beings with equal rights and opportunities next, with potential sponsors casting aside centuries-held images of what women should do. Oh, and if we must stop commenting about your sexual attributes and inclinations, what should we use to divert attention from our own inadequacies?

This is, of course, a tongue-in-cheek response by the (male!) public relations and marketing officer for the Women's Rugby Football Union! It contains many of the most telling criticisms of the media's coverage of women's sport; the performance levels are not perceived to be of the same quality, coverage is minuscule, and therefore sponsorship is paltry, and finally references are made to the sexuality and looks of the participants. Homophobic comments are most likely to occur in sports which do not conform to stereotypical images of femininity, as evidenced by Croft's reference to 'girlie issues'.

Of course, a content analysis of daily newspapers will reveal differences in tenor and tone of reportage in tabloid and broadsheet newspapers but, nevertheless, the general marginalization and trivialization of women's sport by the media has a number of consequences. It:

- diminishes the status of women's sport as a whole
- reinforces the ideology of sport as a masculine domain
- hides role-models from girls
- denies sportswomen's earning power from sponsors
- discourages organizers from staging women's events
- reproduces gender inequities in a powerful way.

The body in question

The relative neglect of women's sport by the media is only one element of the critique. Another is the images of women and women's bodies in media-sport. The promoters of a recent invitational women's golf tournament in Europe admitted that good looks were as important as golfing ability when choosing who to invite to participate. At an international conference in Madrid, in 1990, about social issues in sport, Hargreaves presented a collection of images of women culled from the national press, from commercial advertisements, from soft-porn magazines, and from both fashion and specialist sports magazines. What these images had in common was the depiction of women in sporting environments, dressed in sports clothing or posing with sports equipment, often in sexually provocative or erotic poses. The message was that sports are now part of a culture which commercializes the female body and commercializes sexuality.

Hargreaves (1995) discusses two interrelated elements to this process. The first is the sexualization of female athletes in magazine and press photography, and in sports programmes such as aerobics and keep-fit on TV, where sexuality is implicitly held to be of more interest than sporting ability. Of course, there is plenty of non-sexist treatment of women by the media, where sporting performances are treated seriously, and analysed appropriately. But Hargreaves presents a range of evidence from Europe and North America of the objectification of the female body in sports and an emphasis upon dominant images of femininity. She writes:

> Men tend to be portrayed as physical and aggressive, and their actions and accomplishments are highlighted, whereas women's femininity is symbolised ... through glamorous and sexualised shots, or through implied masculinisation, by the use of informal and intimate names, and by references to athletes' roles as girls, wives, and mothers.

The second element of this commercialization of the female body is the use of sporting images to sell non-sporting products, especially clothes, beauty and health-care products. Erotic sexuality is paramount, the sporting connection is incidental. Pornography also incorporates sporting imagery and sporting props in its eroticization of women.

Who rules, who coaches?

Whitson and McIntosh (1989) discuss two explanations of why women are under-represented in senior technical, administrative volunteer positions in sport. The first and weaker explanation from a functionalist perspective is that women are socialized into particular 'roles', primarily in the domestic or private sphere, and consequently do not tend to volunteer their services. The second explanation is about the power relations between men and women, that the public sphere is more valued than the private, and that men historically have the power to 'define the situation' in the public sphere which best explains the organizational practices and resistance to change in sports organizations.

Cockburn (1991) makes similar points about gendered social processes which give rise to truncated careers for women in non-sporting organizations. In a representative sample of British sports associations, White and Brackenridge (1985) found a marked under-representation of women in the higher policy and decision-making positions, while Hargreaves (1995) notes that in the Sports Council, 1991, there were no women as directors at national or regional levels, or at the National Centres.

A useful exemplar of gender inequity in sports organization is horse-riding – a sport with many girls and women participants. Gregson (1995) notes that the British Show Jumping Association has 16 000 members, many of whom are women, yet the ten-person selection panel for international competitions is exclusively male!

A similar situation occurs in sports coaching, with few women making the senior elite levels. Men are far more likely to coach elite women's sport, than women are to coach elite men's sport. Also women are far more likely than men to find difficulty in reconciling their coaching activity with home and domestic responsibilities. White *et al.* (1990) undertook a qualitative analysis of 'role definitions and conflicts' perceived by women coaches and concluded:

> Women become involved in coaching in response to perceived needs of their sport and out of club loyalty ... many experience difficulties as practising coaches in a male sports culture, where the sporting achievements of women are judged inferior to those of men, and where male coaches are preferred to female coaches by their clients. Conflict is also experienced where women fulfil multiple roles within a sport. The degree of supportiveness of partners was a key factor for women coaches with family responsibilities.

There are of course exceptions in some mixed-sex sports organizations, but there is evidence that a form of **vertical segregation** exists in many sports, with women occupying principally low-status positions, and where coaching female athletes sometimes does not have the same status as coaching male athletes. The Policy Documents of the Sports Council (1994) 'Women and Sport' and of the National Coaching Foundation (1994) 'Women and Coaching' both address these issues:

- there is a male bias in sports culture which often, but not always, downgrades women's involvement as participants and as coaches
- there are not enough women coaches, and women often find difficulty in reconciling their sport involvement with other obligations
- there is a lack of supportive mechanisms to encourage and sustain women's involvement as coaches

- women frequently do not have access to higher levels of coaching.

Strategies for equity

In social science and social policy there are two levels of debate about gender and sport, ranging from a 'surface' or liberal approach about minimizing constraints and equalizing opportunities for women to participate as recreational and/or elite participants, as coaches and as administrators. The second 'deep' or radical level of debate questions the very basis or structure of our sport culture and, of course, the relationships between men and women within it. These two levels of debate are not necessarily mutually exclusive, but might be characterized thus:

- women in sport: inequalities of opportunity
- gender and sport: inequalities of power.

Women in sport: inequalities of opportunity

There is substantial literature on 'women in sport' which has, until quite recently, been concerned with debunking physiological and psychological myths about women, with examining girls' socialization into and out of sport, and the 'role conflicts' which they experience there. Differences and inequities between males and females have been documented with respect to levels of participation, access to funding for women's sports organizations, the selective and sexist nature of the media's treatment of womens' sport, and girls' physical education (Flintoff, 1990; Scraton, 1992).

These strategies are characterized by efforts to increase access to resources, to raise the profile of women, and to equalize opportunity to participate in sports in the public and voluntary sectors. Their major emphasis, therefore, is 'catching up with men', to join in and to access the prevailing sports culture. Equal opportunity objectives, characteristic of most public sector initiatives, are designed to widen the constituency of sport to encompass women more fully and include:

- better facilities
- improved funding
- improved rewards, status, media coverage for outstanding performers
- better coaching (especially male coach/female sportsperson)
- more female coaches
- more representation on local, regional and national bodies
- better understanding of constraints on girls' and women's participation
- better understanding of the influence of parents, teenage culture, school physical education, and the media
- better understanding that gender (a cultural construction) rather than sex (a biological construction) is the most critical influence upon sport participation.

This kind of work has been necessary and useful and is characteristic of most of the current development work for women by sport's organizations. But it does not (indeed is not designed to) address the root causes of gender inequality in sport, let alone whether these play any part in reproducing gender inequalities in society. This approach does *not* therefore ask critical questions about masculine/feminine gender, or about the nature and organization of sport and recreation!

Gender and sport: inequalities of power

The second level is more radical and potentially far-reaching in its consequences, since it represents an attack upon the male-dominated culture of sport, the institutional bases of that power, and the values and practices which sports celebrate and reproduce. Therefore, whereas the first level is to enhance the position of women in sport, the second level questions the whole edifice of the institution of 'sport', examines the causes of gender inequality, and suggests a re-evaluation of play-forms in our culture. This might be achieved by redressing inequalities of power, for women to be able to exert more control over their own bodies, and over the nature and organization of sport and leisure.

Gender can no longer be treated as one of a number of variables that may affect performance (like age, height and weight), or as an issue of sex difference in performance capabilities, or even as a problem of the inequitable distribution of resources, opportunities and experiences upon females and males. Gender is a socially and historically constructed set of power relations (Hargreaves, 1995).

The growth and intervention of feminist scholarship has aimed to understand theoretically the systematic and multidimensional domination of women, and furthermore to develop an agenda for the liberation of women. If women and also enlightened and, as Hargreaves (1990, 1995) has it, 'damaged men' can gain control over their own destinies, then sports would be structured to promote particular human-istic values and eradicate endemic problems such as aggressive competition, chauvinism, sexism, racism, the physical and psychological abuse of athletes, and violence – most of which has been perpetrated by men. The characterization of 'damaged' men is crucial, since this indicates that men are just as much victims of the pressures to conform to stereo-typical images and practices of 'masculinity' as women are to 'femininity' (Messner and Sabo, 1990). This can apply to both men who are, in conventional terms, successful in sport, as it can to those men who have been screened out of sport at an early age because of the overbearing male chauvinism they experience.

The essential contribution, therefore, of a feminist critique of social relationships in sport has been to move from thinking of gender inequality merely in terms of participation, towards an understanding of manifest and historic male advantages and domination in sport. To adapt from Scraton (1987), sport has been constructed by men, for men, where angels fear to tread! The distinction made here between 'surface' and 'deep' levels of feminist strategy to influence sports practice is elaborated upon by Hargreaves (1990), who characterizes sports feminists as:

> Both women and men who share a desire for women to exercise more power and to achieve greater autonomy in sport. It is a desire for change. However, sports feminism is not a unified movement or idea. Some people, for example, argue that male domination should be reduced and that there should be more sports for women modelled on existing traditions, whereas others wish to subvert dominant ideas and to change people's attitudes and actions, and there are groups of women who believe passionately that female sports should be separate from, and qualitatively different from, traditional male sports.

Co-option, separation, cooperation

Drawing together both the surface (equal opportunities) and deep (redistribution of power) debates, the strategic choices available fall into one of the following three categories identified and discussed more fully by Hargreaves (1995):

- **co-option** into a male sphere of activity
- a **separatist** all-female strategy
- a **cooperative** venture with men for qualitative new models of sport/recreation in which differences between the sexes are unimportant.

Cooption is the *equal opportunities* strategy which has been considered earlier as the surface level of debate; women joining men but leaving the culture and structures of sports intact. Moreover, we have seen that, in these cases, women infrequently occupy positions of power and influence in mixed sports organizations. The second and third, more radical, strategies are responses to the acknowledged limitations of the first in tackling the male hegemony of sport.

The advocacy of **separate** women-only sports organizations is a reaction to discriminatory practices and the stereotyping of women. The obvious advantages to this strategy are that women assume control over resources and over decision-making. For those who have experienced sexist behaviour in men's organizations, women-only organizations are likely to be more supportive and enjoyable. However, separatism might sediment gender divisions even further. From separation, difference is an easy step. Male sports institutions are left intact, and there is no need for male sports culture to change even to accommodate women. It is interesting to note that a current trend is for the merging of previously separate men's and women's sports organizations. For example, squash rackets merged in 1989 and hockey will do so in the near future. The third strategy is a **cooperative** venture between women and men for qualitatively new models of sport and recreation. Hargreaves (1990) is in favour of this and quotes Paul Willis approvingly:

> Sport could be presented as a form of activity which emphasises human similarity and not dissimilarity, a form of activity which isn't competitive and measured, a form of activity which expresses values which are indeed unmeasurable, a form of activity which is concerned with individual well-being and satisfaction rather than with comparison. In such a view of sport, differences between the sexes would be unimportant, unnoticed.

This vision of new models of 'sport' necessitates a radical restructuring of sporting practice and organization. Community-oriented initiatives such as 'New Games' (Fleugelman 1976; Leonard, 1976) offer an illustration of what such a future model of sport would be like. Many 'new games' are actually based upon the structures of traditional games, but contain a re-evaluation of what counts as success in their practice, to downplay excessive competitiveness and achievement orientation, to emphasize fun, enjoyment and community. As Fleugelman has it: in 'New Games', if anyone stops enjoying it, you lose. Hargreaves acknowledges this in her reference to a critical comment that 'the only way to reform sport is to convert it into something else that ceases to be sport'! This is, however, whatever your preferences, unlikely to happen in the near future!

Sport and social class

Introduction: the end of class?

This heading is the title of a book by Daniel Bell (1972) in which he assessed technological and attendant socioeconomic change, to predict the diminishing of social class as a key aspect of social relations. Marxist conceptions of two antagonistic classes – one who controls and owns the means of production, the other whose labour is used and exploited in the pursuit of profit – was deemed to be anachronistic. Twenty years later, researchers at the Henley Forecasting Centre came to similar conclusions by depicting Britain in the 1990s as a **mass middle class society** whose consumption patterns, levels of disposable income, and personal identities are becoming more homogeneous.

The economic structure of Britain underwent radical change in the 1980s. As a percentage of GNP, as a source of employment and as a site for investment, the manufacturing sector declined relative to service sector industries such as banking, insurance, retailing, catering and tourism. This shift heralded changes in the nature and quality of work and patterns of class membership; a decline in blue-collar and an increase in white-collar work, a decline in unskilled labour and a demand for technically skilled labour.

Social mobility studies, which are based on comparisons between the present and previous generation's occupations, seem to support this trend; that broadly speaking there is an inter-generational contrast between occupational status, although there is an inherent sexism in this analysis since women's occupations in married households are discounted. The postwar period has witnessed a decline in energy-sapping manual work, the average working week has declined since 1945, car ownership has increased dramatically, and the development of an outdoor and indoor sport and leisure infrastructure is but one manifestation of these general trends – that people have more time and money to exercise consumer choice.

However, general trends as identified by the Henley Forecasting Centre mask considerable differences in the material and cultural resources available to people to exercise choice in sport and leisure. Changes in the nature and availability of employment, and New Right policies in the 1980s to 'roll back the welfare state' (Henry, 1993) and cut public spending, have resulted in greater inequality – a widening gulf between the top and bottom 20% of wage-earners, thereby exacerbating class differences in the ability to 'buy into' sport and leisure. Time for sport and leisure is, however, another critical factor. Many high-earners experience a 'time famine', coping with punishing schedules which leave little time for sport and leisure (Seabrook, 1988), whereas unemployed people have lots of time but little money to spend.

Social surveys

The General Household Survey has established a relationship between levels and types of sports participation and social class as measured by occupation. Overall participation rates are highest for professional workers and lowest for unskilled manual workers (Table 8.1), although some sports, such as soccer, snooker and darts, are most popular with junior non-manual and manual socioeconomic groups. The Central Statistical Office (1995) also indicates that sports participation declines across the

Table 8.1 Participation[1] in sports, games and physical activities by socioeconomic group[2], 1993–94 (percentage)

	Professional	Employers and managers	Intermediate and junior non-manual	Skilled manual and own account non-professional	Semi-skilled manual and personal service	Unskilled manual	All socio-economic groups[3]
Walking	57	46	42	39	36	31	41
Swimming	27	19	18	10	11	8	15
Snooker/pool/billiards	11	12	8	17	10	9	12
Keep fit/yoga	13	12	18	6	9	8	12
Cycling	14	9	9	10	8	9	10
Darts	6	5	4	8	6	6	6
Weight lifting/training	7	5	5	6	4	3	5
Golf	9	10	5	6	2	2	5
Running/jogging	11	6	4	3	2	2	5
Soccer	6	3	3	6	3	3	4

[1] Percentage participating in the four weeks before interview.
[2] Socioeconomic group is based on the person's current or most recent job.
[3] Includes full-time students, members of the armed forces, those who have never worked and those whose job was inadequately described.

Source: Social Trends 26, 1996. Crown Copyright 1996. Reproduced by permission of the Controller of HMSO and the Office for National Statistics.

classes. For example, professional and managerial groups are twice as likely to play in team sports as those people in the unskilled manual group.

The Sports Council primarily use age and sex as the basis for their planning decisions about facility provision, but recently the council commissioned a research project to assess the impact of social class membership on sports participation in the three categories of individual, hall and pitch sports. Reporting on this project, Coalter *et al.* (1995) noted that the specific concern was to assess 'additionality' – the increase in the ability to predict sports participation when social class is combined with the variables of age and sex. Table 8.2 shows the extent to which social class, as well as age and sex, explain the variance in participation/non-participation in individual sports. A key finding is that the influence of social class varies substantially between these individual sports.

Table 8.2 Individual sports and the variance explained by age, sex, and social class

	Age only	*Sex only*	*Social class only*
	Percentage variance explained		
Keep fit/aerobics	40.0	32.8	27.9
Swimming (outdoor)	59.1	2.3	26.1
Golf	22.7	50.4	15.4
Swimming (indoor)	75.7	3.5	10.1
Badminton	65.7	5.1	8.8
Cycling	47.9	20.2	6.9
Jogging	66.2	17.1	7.6
Ten pin bowling	75.5	8.1	5.0
Snooker/pool	51.3	38.5	4.5
Weight training	61.0	27.1	3.2
Hall sports	74.4	3.2	18.3

Source: Coalter *et al.* (1995), by permission.

One of their key findings, however, is that educational level appears to be the most important component of social class for influencing participation/non-participation. There is a strong statistical relationship between educational qualifications and social class (69% of social class I have a degree compared with 0.4% from social class VI), and they note that participation rates for graduates, in a sample of indoor and outdoor sports, are more than double those with no qualifications. Coalter and co-workers observe that:

> Those who remain in full-time education after the statutory leaving age are more likely to have the free time and to be provided with the opportunity for free participation in a wide range of sports. This longer period of 'independence' permits the development of a longer term commitment to participation, and the willingness to protect it in the face of work and relationship commitments.

You might still, however, doubt the importance of social class as a key factor in explaining sport participation. Whippet-racing might be essentially a working-class pursuit, whereas polo is essentially an upper-class activity – but most mainstream sports would seem to be readily accessible elements of popular culture. This relative accessibility is evident in the Sports Council's policy credo of 'Sport for All' which seems to be both a reasonable and laudable aim. A parallel 'Art for All' policy has not been developed by the Arts Council which seems to suggest that the cultural competences required for sport, unlike high art, are more or less equally distributed among the population. But you must ask yourself ... which sports ... for whom ... and in which places? Are all sports equally accessible and, if not, is it merely a difference in the relative cost of activities, or are some sports **socially exclusive**, even if not **cost exclusive**? These two terms suggest that social class has not only economic but also cultural dimensions.

Dimensions of class

It is difficult to classify various occupations un-equivocally into particular class categories, but occupation is only one criterion which is used by people in determining social class. It is useful there-fore to conceive of (more) objective and (more) subjec-tive dimensions of social class, both of which have real effects on sports participation.

The **objective dimension** is about a person's posi-tion in the labour market as indicated by paid occu-pation, an important element of social stratification. Occupation correlates closely with income, life-chances, lifestyle, where one lives, and social networks at both work and in leisure time. There are some inconsistencies in this (Luschen, 1984). For example, an individual with a high level of education and in a recognized profession with a relatively high social status might have a low income (e.g. a minister of religion) and vice versa. However, all social surveys of sport and leisure participation do use occupation as the prime indicator of social class.

The **subjective dimension** relates to people's different and partial perceptions of class structure – which we can term **class-imagery**. Whatever the objective reality of inequalities deriving from occupa-tional position, people have different images or models of this reality. For example, in a recent National Opinion Poll survey, respondents were asked which of the following were important in their percep-tion of other people's social class membership: the way they speak, where they live, the friends they have, their job, the sort of school they went to, the way they spend their money, the amount of money they have, the way they dress, the car they own. Note that the first five of these indicate the social networks in which people live, whereas the last four are primarily about consumption patterns.

The complex meanings and indicators of social class underline the limitations of social surveys such as the General Household Survey (see Table 8.1). Statistical information on class membership of sports is the result of fairly simple survey work using questionnaires and interviewing as the method of data collection, in an attempt to provide 'social facts' about people's behaviour. These methods – and the statistics which are a derivative – tell us 'who does what' but provide little insight into the complex social dynamics through which people (according to their class membership) invest activities with particular meanings, adopt particular styles, choose public or private spaces, choose playful or more serious modes of participation, choose the people they play sports with, or choose particular sports because of their social image.

The dynamics of choice in sport

One of the key issues for sociology is to establish and examine the interrelationships or social dynamics between the objective and the subjective – between the social structure (labour market situation) and the pattern of class imagery. The analysis by Bourdieu and his co-researchers (1978, 1985) provides rich insights into these complex social dynamics and provides compelling evidence for the saliency of social class as a mediator of choice for sport. The basis of Bourdieu's account is his Theory of (Individual) Practice which stresses the importance of early socialization in structuring if not determining a person's choice and preferences in sport. On this basis, he develops a fascinating explanation of people's differing perceptions of the economic, physical and, most crucially, *cultural* costs and benefits of participation in the range of sports on offer. His magnus opus is entitled 'Distinction', which refers to his central theme: that the main factors governing choice in sport are social rather than physical – a concern by dominant groups to pursue distinctive sports in distinctive (i.e. private) places, inaccessible either economically or culturally to other social classes.

The following summarizes the key elements of Bourdieu's analysis, although the reader is directed towards the more extensive and critical assessment provided by Jarvie and Maguire (1994).

The habitus

Bourdieu argues that early childhood socialization experiences and conditionings, and the social networks within which these are gained, have a crucial effect upon an individual's outlook, attitudes and values, dispositions, tastes, and preferences in sport, in art, in clothing styles, home decor, and in all other aspects of cultural participation and consumption. This is what he calls 'the habitus' – a matrix of lasting transposable dispositions or way of seeing and evaluating the world which influences an individual's tastes and preferences in all activities. Since the habitus is developed unconsciously or tacitly, mainly in informal family and immediate social circles, it is experienced as natural, as taken-for-granted. Bourdieu's central thesis therefore is that a person's interests in and perceptions of the different types of sport and their social settings, if not *determined* by one's upbringing, are crucially related to early socialization. This, in turn, gives rise to the meanings and values a person holds, his/her evaluation of sport in terms of personal identity and the place of sport in one's lifestyle (Sack, 1988).

Cultural capital

On this basis, Bourdieu suggests that each individual possesses 'cultural capital' – a product of specific class-based lifestyles. As is the case with economic capital, cultural capital is an asset which can be acquired and invested. We tend to think that the more something costs, the more socially exclusive it is, the more 'distinctive'. Bourdieu, however, goes beyond this crude measurement, pointing out that there is no simple correspondence between middle/working-class involvement in sports and high/low cost. For example, rambling is a relatively cheap sport or recreation, but the profile of the Ramblers' Association in Britain is resolutely middle-class. Similarly, how do you account for the different class composition of hockey and soccer? Arguably, both cost about the same, require similar expenditure of energy, and comparable time in preparation and training.

Bourdieu (1985) argues, therefore, that explanations of differential participation in sport cannot be simply related to how expensive they are, nor to the amount of disposable income of individuals. He suggests that sports are distinguished in terms of the nature and extent of **cultural** capital required or gained. He writes:

> To understand the class distribution of the various sports, one would have to take account of the representation which, in terms of their specific schemes of perception and appreciation, the different classes have of the costs (economic, cultural, and physical) and benefits attached to the different sports.

Physical benefits might be immediate or deferred, visible (e.g. body-building) or less visible (e.g. jogging), or primarily about health, beauty, strength or suppleness. Economic and cultural benefits include assessments of the association of a sport with a particular class grouping (e.g. boxing with the working class, golf with the middle class), and access to socially exclusive groups. Anyone who has felt uncomfortable or 'out of place' in a sport setting (e.g. a private golf club) will have experienced the degree of social closure which can operate in some sport settings.

Cultural capital is easy to understand in terms of 'high' arts such as opera, painting and classical music. Here, patronage is related to the requisite knowledge and ability to appreciate the subtleties of performance or artefact, much of which stems from early exposure to this culture. It is perhaps more difficult to appreciate with respect to sport, but Bourdieu stresses that the habitus operates in all areas of culture, so that tastes and preferences in art are linked to those in sport and elsewhere.

Sport as a 'field of stylistic possibles'

The practice of sport provides choices to be made on the basis of social class. Bourdieu (1985) invites us to conceive of sports as 'an objectively instituted field of stylistic possibles'. This applies to any field of consumerism and cultural practice, e.g. cars, news-papers, holiday resorts, design or furnishing of house and garden, drinks. All of these (like sports) provide a small number of distinctive features which allow the most fundamental **social** differences to be expressed. Notions of disinterestedness, refinement and control, says Bourdieu, typify 'bourgeois' or middle-class sport involvement, the privileged classes tending to treat the body as an end in itself. The emphasis is on the **intrinsic** functioning of the body and on its appearance. Bourdieu's observations about 'jogging' and other strictly health-orientated practices are instructive here.

Jogging is only meaningful in relation to a theoretical abstract knowledge of the effects of exercise. It presupposes a faith in deferred and intangible profits from exercise for its own sake, as contrasted with the practical-oriented movements of everyday life. Bourdieu has much to say about the macro-biotic health cult as an example of the 'bourgeois aesthetic' in practical action. In contrast, working-class involvement in sport tends to be typified by instrumentality, by function rather than form. There is a tendency for working-class groups to express an **instrumental** relation to the body, often choosing sports which require large investments of effort.

Certain sports then are 'predisposed' for use by certain groups (identified by their class habitus). One of the primary lines of fracture discussed by Bourdieu is that between individual sports and team sports (which for Bourdieu encapsulate 'pure' and 'barbarous' taste, respectively). Many popular team sports only require bodily and cultural competences that are fairly equally distributed between classes and are therefore relatively accessible. Their accessibility and consequent lack of distinction tends to discredit them in the eyes of privileged groups. They

> ... combine all the features which repel the dominant class; not only the social composition of their public which redoubles their commonness but also the values and virtues demanded, strength, endurance, violence, sacrifice, docility, submission to collective discipline, and the exaltation of competition.

In contrast to team sports, individual sports display all the features which appeal to the 'dominant' taste. They are more free in that they are (often) practised in exclusive places at times one chooses and with chosen partners. They require relatively low physical exertion (or at least such exertion is freely determined), but need a relatively high investment of time and (early) learning. These sports age well, i.e. are (relatively) independent of variations in bodily capital. They give rise to highly ritualized competitions governed by canons of acceptable behaviour (fair play) beyond the codified rules. The sporting exchanges take on the air of a highly controlled social exchange, excluding all physical or verbal violence, shouting, and wild gestures and direct contact between the opponents.

Bourdieu's general proposition here is that a sport is more likely to be adopted or appropriated by a particular social class if it does *not* contradict that class's relation to the body at its deepest level. This extended discussion of team and individual sports does not do justice to the subtlety of Bourdieu's thesis. He also considers:

- oppositions either within sports (e.g. expensive/cheap ways of participating)
- between sports (e.g. expensive versus cheap individual sports)
- oppositions between 'manly high energy sports' (e.g. soccer, rugby), 'introverted self-expressive sports' (e.g. yoga) and 'cybernetic sports' (e.g. motor-racing).

Figure 8.1 summarizes these points.

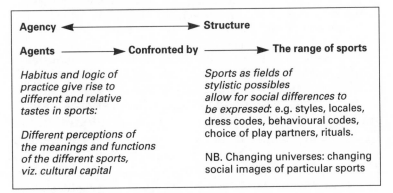

Figure 8.1 Sport as fields of taste

Distributional significance

Bourdieu (1985) suggests that sports have different class-related 'images' and argues that the social image of sports cuts across the intrinsic benefits a sport might possess. Consider, for example, two sports which are similar in structure and have similar intrinsic/health and fitness benefits yet attract a different spectrum of participants, e.g. golf and bowls, or rugby union and soccer. Bourdieu accounts for the varying social image of different sports in terms of their '**distributional significance**' (Figure 8.2). The social significance of different sports derives from their varying distribution among people who themselves are distributed in class groupings, i.e. their class imagery. As noted earlier, social images of particular sports might be sustained long after a change in their relative accessibility in cost terms. A key point therefore in Bourdieu's analysis is that the influence of social class in sport cannot simply be reduced to how expensive they are for participants. Rather, sports have a 'positional value' deriving from their social accessibility.

Agency ◄─────────────► Structure	
Agents	*Sports*
Individuals, on the basis of their habitus, vary in the meanings and functions they ascribe to sports	Sports have a distributional significance: their social image derives from their distribution among agents who are themselves distributed in social space

Figure 8.2 Distributional significance of sports

The pursuit of distinction

Sports are inequitably distributed across the social class spectrum, leading to various promotional and marketing strategies. Bourdieu's (1985) analysis, however, indicates the limitations of such an approach, and the consequences if such campaigns are successful. Consider a fairly 'up-market' sport, by which we mean a sport which is both relatively cost-exclusive and relatively socially-exclusive. Further, suppose that promotional campaigns are so successful that the activity is popularized, and that therefore its social exclusiveness is diminished. According to Bourdieu's analysis, that activity then ceases to be distinctive and is therefore 'deserted' by the original adherents or they seek more distinctive (i.e. private and exclusive) spaces.

A classic historical example is soccer. Until 1882, the FA Cup was won by amateur southern teams mainly comprised of ex-public schoolboys. The game became popularized and from 1882 onwards the FA Cup was won by professional and predominantly working-class northern teams, starting with Blackburn Rovers. The consequence of this popularization was a desertion of the amateur middle-class players either into their own (private and therefore distinctive) competitions such as the Arthur Dunn Cup or to other sports (e.g. Rugby Union).

For Bourdieu (1985), sports are 'an endless play of self-relativising tastes'. Tastes or choice of sport are relative and, in fact, *distastes* of other tastes, to be understood as social *breaks*.[1] Noting the interconnections between sport, social fields and class relations, Jarvie and Maguire (1994) cite a key passage from Bourdieu (1978):

> Sport like any other practice, is an object of struggles between the fractions of the dominant class[2] and also between the social classes ... the field of sporting practices is the site of struggles in which what is at stake ... is the monopolistic capacity to impose the legitimate definition of sporting practice.

We live in a **class-conscious** society, even though this is seldom overtly acknowledged. Bourdieu's analysis provides a detailed explanation of how class operates with respect to all forms of cultural activity. Statistical information about the distribution of sport according to the Registrar-General's classification of

[1] Warde (1995) has carried out a fascinating analysis of weekly food consumption in Britain, informed by Bourdieu's perspectives on taste cultures. He demonstrates the existence of significant and different 'communities of taste' between employers, professionals, the self-employed, routine white collar workers and the manual working class.

[2] The fractions of the **dominant** class include the dominant fraction (those richest in economic capital, such as a self-made businessman), and the **dominated** fraction (those richest in cultural capital, such as academics).

social class does not begin to explain some of the complex social mechanisms which 'filter' people in and out of different sports, and determine the values and attitudes which individual participants adopt. Hargreaves' (1986) analysis of working-class culture complements Bourdieu's thesis by showing how working-class people can be screened out of positions in sports organizations. Drawing on a number of community studies, Hargreaves shows that sports continue to mark a 'cultural boundary' among working-class people. Noting class differentiation in sport and recreation, he provides an explanation of this difference and inequality by suggesting that in both the voluntary and the public sector 'middle-class norms' act against working-class involvement. He further acknowledges that 'the working classes' have been transformed in the last three decades, leading to divisions within this social class in their attitude towards, and involvement in, sport.

British Sports Council policy, with reference to the effect of social class, is poorly articulated except for specific measures aimed at unemployed people and inner-city sports development initiatives. However, it should now be clear that sports might be either/both cost-exclusive and/or socially-exclusive, and that this inequality is intimately connected with factors such as occupation, car-ownership, disposable income, early socialization influences (family and immediate social circle) and with the 'image' of specific sports. A key question is '**in what ways do sports restrict the involvement of certain social classes, and what action might be taken to redress such disadvantages**'?

An underclass?

Because of a lack of paid occupation and their in-visibility in the labour market, unemployed people are conventionally labelled an 'underclass'. This term is used in recognition of the status associated with paid employment. However, this is an imprecise label since it suggests that most unemployed people originate in working-class occupations. The relative decline of manufacturing industry in Britain in the 1970s and early 1980s disadvantaged occupational groupings conventionally termed 'working class' – but witness, for example, the number of advertising executives, financiers and architects out of work in the early 1990s.

According to Glyptis (1991), the sport and leisure prospects for the unemployed are limited by low incomes, loss of social contacts and status, and a loss of confidence brought about by the perceived stigma of being out of work. Most public sector facilities and voluntary sports organizations have pricing/membership policies which take account of unemployment – the term 'unwaged' is more accurate. In contrast to busy people identified by the Sports Council (1988) who experience a 'time famine', unwaged people have an abundance of 'free time' but are denied not only the income, but also the activity and sources of social interaction, identity and status which paid occupations provide.[3]

Class rules

The influence of social class on sport is much more difficult to understand than the more obvious differences between people on the basis of age, gender or ability. The reason is that we do not all operate with the same conceptions of social class. Therefore, objective measures (in terms of paid occupation) need to be supplemented by more subjective connotations of class-imagery. Bourdieu's (1985) analysis is an

[3] For a more extensive analysis, read Stokes (1983).

explanation of how this imagery works out in practice. In particular, he illustrates the limitations of campaigns to popularize particular sports, and also argues that people's perceptions, values and dispositions regarding sport are relative to their class position.

Both Bourdieu and feminist perspectives indicate the critical influence of socialization practices on participation in sport, but Bourdieu says little about gender-divisions and you need to ask yourself how his analysis relates to or contradicts the perspective provided in Chapter 7. Hargreaves (1986) considers the disjunction between working-class popular culture and traditional sports organizations. People from higher occupational groupings have more active and more varied sporting lifestyles, and are much more likely to be in the positions of power within sports organizations. The challenge is to make all sporting roles – participation, coaching, organizing, and administrating – more accessible and less socially exclusive.

Summary

The main aim of Part Two of this book has been to address the social divisions which permeate and influence all levels and types of sport in society. This is premissed upon an implicit acknowledgement that participation in sport – as participant, coach and administrator – should be available to everyone. On the other hand, in each of the four chapters it has been argued that the structure and culture of sports organizations are unrepresentative of the British population. Sports have clearly been democratized beyond the narrow confines of the middle-class elite who contoured the early development of modern sports, but constraints on participation arising from structural inequality remain.

Sports provision has become an element of social

policy in the last twenty years, and a principal concern has been to increase access and opportunity among non-participants and infrequent participants. Elite sports are encouraged to seek support from the private sector, but the limitations of a market-driven approach have been acknowledged.

More recently, however, sociological perspectives have been developed which indicate continued inequity. People in positions of power and influence within sports organizations are encouraged to examine their own practice in a critical manner. Development work, based on an understanding that traditional sports practice reproduces social inequality, seeks ways in which sport might be democratized in an otherwise inegalitarian society.

References

Abercrombie, N. (1984) *Dictionary of Sociology*, Penguin Books, Harmondsworth, UK.

Abrams, J. & Wolsey, C. (1996) Organisational change and the non-profit making sports sector in the UK. *World Leisure and Recreation Association Conference*, Cardiff, 15–20 July.

Allen, D. and Fahey, B. (eds) (1982) *Being Human in Sport*, Lea and Febiger, Philadelphia.

Appadurai, A. (1990) Disjuncture and difference in the global cultural economy. *Theory, Culture and Society*, **7**, 295–311.

Arnold, P. (1979) *Meaning in Movement, Sport, and Physical Education*, Heinemann, London.

Beamish, R. (1982) Sport and the logic of capitalism. In *Sport, Culture and the Modern State* (eds R. Gruneau and H. Cantelon), University of Toronto Press.

Becker, H. (1984) *Artworlds*, University of California Press, Los Angeles.

Bell, D. (1972) *The Coming of Post-Industrial Society*, Penguin Books, Harmondsworth, UK.

Birkett, D. (1993) Women: this sporting strife. *The Guardian*, 16 Nov.

Bishop, J. and Hoggett, P. (1986) *Organising Around Enthusiasms; Mutual Aid in Leisure.* Comedia, London.

Borrett, N., Kew, F. and Stockham, K. (1995) Disabled young people: opportunities and constraints for sport and leisure. *Papers in Community Studies*, no. 8, Bradford and Ilkley College.

Bourdieu, P. (1978) Sport and social class. *Social Science Information*, **18**(6), 821–830.

Bourdieu, P. (1985) *Distinction: A Social Critique of the Judgement of Taste*, Routledge, London.

Brackenridge, C. (1991) Cross-gender coaching

relationships: myth, drama, or crisis. *Coaching Focus*, **16**, 12–13.

Brailsford, D. (1988) *Bareknuckles: A Social History of Prizefighting*, Lutterworth, Cambridge.

Brailsford, D. (1992) *British Sport: A Social History*, Lutterworth Press, Cambridge.

Brohm, J.-M., (1978) *Sport: A Prison of Measured Time*, Ink Links, London.

Brown, A. (1987) *Active Games for Children with Movement Problems*, Harper & Row, London.

Caillois, R. (1961) *Man, Play, and Games*, Free Press, New York.

Cain, N. (1995) Player power. *Rugby News*, September 10–15.

Carrington, B. (1983) Sport as a sidetrack. In *Race, Class and Education*, (eds L. Barton, and S. Walker), Croom Helm, London.

Carroll, B. (1993) Factors influencing ethnic minority groups participation in sport. *Physical Education Review*, **16**(1), 55–66.

Cashmore, E. (1982) *Black Sportsmen*, RKP, London.

Cashmore, E. (1991) *Making Sense of Sport*, Routledge, London.

Central Statistical Office (1995) *Social Trends*, No. 25, HMSO, London.

Clarke, A. and Clarke, J. (1982) Highlights and action replays: ideology, sport and the media. In *Sport, Culture and Ideology* (ed. J. Hargreaves), RKP, London.

Clarke, A. and Critcher, C. (1985) *The Devil Makes Work*, Macmillan, London.

Cleary, M. (1995) Bras not for burning on banks of the Thames. *The Observer*, 26 March.

Coakley, J. (1986) *Sport in Society: Issues and Controversies*, Kingston Press, London.

Coakley, J. (1992) Burn-out amongst adolescent athletes. *Sociology of Sport*, **3**, 271–285.

Coalter, F., Dowers, S. and Baxter, M. (1995) The impact of social class and education on sports participation: some evidence from the General

Household Survey. In *Leisure and Social Stratification* (ed. K. Roberts), Leisure Studies Association, University of Brighton, Eastbourne.

Cockburn, C. (1991) *In the Way of Women: Men's Resistance to Sex Equality in Organisations*, Macmillan, London.

Critcher, C. (1979) Football since the war. In *Working Class Culture* (eds J. Clarke *et al.*), Hutchinson, London.

Critcher, C. (1984) Review essay of *Blowing the Whistle: The Politics of Sport* (by G. Whannel). *Leisure Studies*, **3**, 246–247.

Critcher, C., Bramham, P. and Tomlinson, A. (1996) *Sociology of Leisure: A Reader*, E. & F. Spon, London.

Croft, I. (1993) Come on girls, play the game! *The Guardian*, 2 April.

Csikszentmihalyi, M. (1975) *Beyond Boredom and Anxiety*, Jossey Bass, San Francisco.

Csikszentmihalyi, M. (1992) *Flow: The Psychology of Happiness*, Ryder Press, London.

D'Agostino, F. (1981) The ethos of games. *Journal of Philosophy of Sport*, **8**, 7–8.

Davis, L. (1993) Critical analysis of popular media and the concept of ideal subject position. *Quest*, **45**, 165–181.

Dewar, A. (1993) Would all the generic women in sport please stand up? Challenges facing feminist sport sociology. *Quest*, **45**, 211–229.

Duncan, M. (1990) Sport photos and sexual difference: images of men and women in the 1984 and 1988 Olympics. *Sociology of Sport Journal*, **7**(1), 22–43

Duncan, M. and Brummett, B. (1987) The mediation of spectator sport. *Research Quarterly*, **58**(2), 74–96.

Dunning, E. and Sheard, K. (1979) *Barbarians, Gentlemen, and Players*, Martin Robertson, Oxford.

Edwards, H. (1973) *Sociology of Sport*, Dorsey Press, New York.

Eichberg, H. (1984) Olympic sport: neo-colonialization and alternatives. *International Review for Sociology of Sport*, **19**(1), 97–106.

Elias, N. and Dunning, E. (1986) *Quest for Excitement: Sport and Leisure in the Civilizing Process*, Basil Blackwell, Oxford.

Fairchild, D. (1994) From the mountains to the valleys: theorizing gender in sport. *Quest*, **46**, 369–384.

Fejgin, N. (1994) Participation in high school competitive sport: a subversion of school mission or contribution to academic goals. *Sociology of Sport Journal*, **11**(3), 211–230.

Fine, G. (1987) *With the Boys: Little League Baseball and Pre-adolescent Culture*, University of Chicago Press.

Fleming, S. (1990) Sport, schooling and South Asian youth culture. *Sport, Racism and Ethnicity* (ed. G. Jarvie), Falmer Press, London.

Fleming, S. (1994) Sport and South Asian youth: the perils of false universalism and stereotyping. *Leisure Studies*, **13**, 159–177.

Fleugelman, A. (1976) *The New Games Book*, Doubleday, New York.

Flintoff, A. (1990) Physical education, equal opportunities and the National Curriculum. *Physical Education Review*, **13**(2), 85–100.

Fraleigh, W. (1984) *Right Actions in Sport*, Human Kinetics, Champaign, Illinois.

French, C. and Raven, D. (1959) The bases of power. In *Studies in Social Power* (ed. D. Cartwright), Institute for Social Research, London.

Fryer, P. (1993) *The History of Black People in Britain*, Pluto Press, London.

Glyptis, S. (1991) Local authority provision for the unemployed. *International Review of Sociology of Sport*, **26**(2), 101–118.

Goldlust, J. (1987) *Playing For Keeps: Sports, the Media and Society*, Longmans, Cheshire.

Gregson, J. (1995) Saddling up to sexism. *The Observer*, 16 April.

Gruneau, R. (1983) *Class, Sports, and Social Development*, University of Massachussetts Press, Amherst.

Gurevitch, M. (1991) The globalization of electronic journalism. In *Mass Media and Society*, (eds J. Curran and M. Gurevitch), Arnold, London.

Guttmann, A. (1978) *From Ritual to Record*, Columbia University Press, New York.

Hall, A. (1990) How should we theorize gender in the context of sport. In *Sport, Men and the Gender Order* (eds M. Messner and D. Sabo), Human Kinetics, Champaign, Illinois.

Hallinan, C. (1991) Aborigines and positional segregation in Australian rugby league. *International Review of Sociology of Sport*, **26**(2), 69–82.

Hargreaves, John (1986) *Sport, Power, and Culture*, Polity, Oxford.

Hargreaves, Jen. (1987) Sport, TV and the economic imperative. *New Students Magazine*, March, 40–42.

Hargreaves, Jen. (1990) Gender on the sports agenda. *International Review of Sociology of Sport*, **25**(4), 287–308.

Hargreaves, Jen. (1995) *Sporting Females: Critical Issues in the History and Sociology of Women's Sport*, Routledge and Kegan Paul, London.

Harper, W. (1993) Just sport. *Quest*, **45**, 448–459.

Hart, M. (ed.) (1976) *Sport in the Socio-cultural Process*, W. C. Brown, Dubuque, Iowa.

Haywood, L., Kew, F., Bramham, P. *et al.* (1995) *Understanding Leisure*, Stanley Thornes, Cheltenham.

Heikkala, J. (1991) Elite athletes: competition and co-operation; some philosophical and ethical problems. *International Seminar on Sport, Social Change, and Social Process*, Tallinn, Estonia, 26–29 June.

Henderson, K. (1995) Women with physical disabilities and the negotiation of leisure constraints. *Leisure Studies*, **14**(4), 17–31.

Henry, I. (1993) *The Politics of Leisure Policy*, Macmillan, London.

HMSO (1989) *Building on Ability: Sport for People with Disabilities*, Report of the Minister of Sport's Review Group, HMSO, London.

HMSO (1991) *The National Curriculum*, Final Report of the Physical Education Working Group, HMSO, London.

Hoberman, J. (1992) *Mortal Engines: The Science of Performance and the Dehumanization of Sport*, Free Press, New York.

Hoffman, S. (1992) *Sport and Religion*, Human Kinetics, Champaign, Illinois.

Hughes, R. and Coakley, J. (1991) Positive deviance amongst athletes: the implications of over-conformity to the Sport Ethic. *Sociology of Sport Journal*, **8**(4), 307–325.

Huizinga, J. (1972) *Homo Ludens: A Study of the Play Element in Culture*, Beacon Press, Boston. Originally published 1938.

Hunt, R. (1993) Down but not out. *The Leisure Manager*, February, 13–15.

Jarvie, G. (ed.) (1990) *Sport, Racism and Ethnicity*, Falmer Press, London.

Jarvie, G. and Maguire, J. (1994) *Sport and Leisure in Social Thought*, Routledge, London.

Jowsey, S. (1992) *Can I Play Too? PE for Physically Disabled Children in Mainstream Schools*, David Fulton, London.

Kane, M. (1971) An assessment of black is best. *Sports Illustrated*, **34**(3), 78–83.

Kew, F. (1987) Contested rules. *International Review for Sociology of Sport*, **22**(2), 125–35.

Kew, F. (1990) The development of games: an endogenous explanation. *International Review of Sociology for Sport*, **25**(4), 251–267.

Kleinman, S. (1982) The significance of movement: a phenomenological approach. In *Sport and the Body* (ed. E. Gerber), Lea and Febiger, Philadelphia.

Lasch, C. (1979) *The Culture of Narcissism*, Warner Books, New York.

Lashley, H. (1991) Blacks in sport: opportunity or control? In *Social Scientific Perspectives on Sport* (ed. F. Kew), National Coaching Foundation, Leeds.

Lavoie, M. (1989) Stacking, performance differentials and salary discrimination in professional ice hockey. *Sociology of Sport Journal*, **6**(1), 17–35.

Leamon, O. and Carrington, B. (1985) Athleticism and the reproduction of gender and ethnic marginality. *Leisure Studies*, **4**(2), 205–218.

Leonard, G. (1976) *The Ultimate Athlete*, Viking Press, New York.

Leonard, W. (1990) Centrality of position and managerial recruitment: the case of major league baseball. *Sociology of Sport Journal*, **7**(3), 294–301.

Luschen, G. (1970) Co-operation, association, and contest. *Journal of Conflict Resolution*, **14**, 21–24.

Luschen, G. (1984) Status crystallization, social class, integration, and sport. *International Review for Sociology of Sport*, **19**(3–4), 283–294.

McIntosh, P. (1979) *Fair Play: Ethics in Sport and Education*, Heinemann, London.

MacIntyre, A. (1981) *After Virtue*, Duckworth, London.

Maguire, J. (1988) The commercialisation of English elite basketball 1972–88: a figurational perspective. *International Review for Sociology of Sport*, **23–24**, 305–325.

Maguire, J. (1990) Race and position assignment in British professional soccer. In *Sport, Racism and Ethnicity* (ed. G. Jarvie), Falmer Press, London.

Maguire, J. (1991) The commercialisation of sport and athletes' rights. In *Social Scientific Perspectives on Sport* (ed. F. Kew), National Coaching Foundation, Leeds.

Marshall, H. (1931) An inquisition on British sport. *The Listener*, 1 July, suppl. no.14.

Marshall, T. (1983) Integration of the disabled into sport. University of Birmingham (unpublished).

Marshall, T. (1991) Report on 'building on ability'. *Sport and Leisure*, May/June, 14–15.

Mason, T. (1988) *Sport in Britain*, Faber and Faber, London.

Meaden, C. (1996) *The Profile System*. Information Sheet No. 20, British Sports Association for the Disabled, May.

Messner, M. and Sabo, D. (1990) *Sport, Men and the Gender Order*, Human Kinetics, Champaign, Illinois.

Metheny, E. (1976) The symbolic power of sport. In *Sport and the Body* (ed. E. Gerber), Lea and Febiger, New York.

Morgan, W. (1984) Social philosophy of sport: a critical interpretation. *Journal of Philosophy of Sport*, **10**, 33–51.

National Coaching Foundation (1994) *Women and Coaching: Policy and Action Plan*, National Coaching Foundation, Leeds.

Nelson, M. (1991) *Are We Winning Yet? How Women are Changing Sports and Sports are Changing Women*, Randon House, New York.

Novak, J. (1976) *The Joy of Sports: End Zones, Baskets, Balls, and the Consecration of the American Spirit*, Basic Books, New York.

O'Regan, J. (1995) One game? *Rugby News*, September, 26–27.

Pearson, K. (1979) *Surfing Sub-cultures in Australia and New Zealand*, Queensland University Press, St. Lucia.

Rail, G. (1990) Physical contact in women's basketball: a phenomenological analysis. *International Review for Sport Sociology*, **27**(1), 1–26.

Ravizza, K. (1982) Potential of the sports experience. In *Being Human in Sport* (eds D. Allen and B. Fahey), Lea and Febiger, Philadelphia.

Rigauer, B. (1982) *Sport and Work*, Columbia University Press, New York.

Rowe, D. and Brown, P. (1994) Promoting women's sport: theory policy and practice. *Leisure Studies*, **13**, 97–110.

Sack, H. (1988) Relationship between sport involvement and life-style in youth cultures. *International Review for Sociology of Sport*, **23**(3), 213–232.

Sargent, P. (1987) Equal access to leisure. *Leisure Management*, August, 53–56.

Schneider, A. and Butcher, R. (1993) For the love of the game: a philosophical defence of amateurism. *Quest*, **45**, 460–469.

Scott, J. (1981) *The Athletic Revolution*, Free Press, New York.

Scraton, S. (1987) Boys muscle in where angels fear to tread. Girls' sub-culture and physical activities. In *Sport, Leisure and Social Relations* (eds J. Horne, D. Jary and A. Tomlinson), Routledge and Kegan Paul, London.

Scraton, S. (1992) *Shaping Up to Womanhood: Gender, Girls and Physical Education*, Open University Press, Milton Keynes.

Seabrook, J. (1988) *The Leisure Society*, Blackwell, Oxford.

Sewart, J. (1987) The commodification of sport. *International Review for Sociology of Sport*, **22**(3), 171–188.

Snyder, E. and Spreitzer, E. (1978) *Social Aspects of Sport*, Prentice-Hall, New Jersey.

Sports Council (1988) *Into the '90's: A Strategy for Sport 1988–1993*, The Sports Council, London.

Sports Council (1993) *Sport and People with Disabilities – Guidelines for Governing Bodies of Sport*, The Sports Council, London.

Sports Council (1994) *Women and Sport*, The Sports Council, London.

Stead, G. and Swain, G. (1990) *Youthwork and Sport*, National Youth Bureau, Leicester.

Stebbins, R. (1993) Stacking in professional American football: implications for the Canadian game. *International Review for Sociology of Sport*, **28**(1), 65–74.

Stokes, G. (1983) Work, unemployment and leisure. *Leisure Studies*, **2**, 3.

Stone, G. (1970) American sports: play and display. In *Sport and Society: An Anthology* (eds J. Talamini and C. Page), Little, Brown, Boston. Originally published 1955.

Vaz, E. (1977) Institutionalised rule violation in professional hockey: perspectives and control systems. *Journal of the Canadian Association of Health, PE, and Recreation,* **43**(3), 6–14.

Warde, A. (1995) Cultural change and class differentiation: distinction and taste in the British middle classes 1968–88. In *Leisure and Social Stratification* (ed. K. Roberts), Leisure Studies Association, University of Brighton, Eastbourne.

Wedderburn, M. (1990) *You're Black, You're Fast, You're on the Wing,* MA thesis, Loughborough University (unpublished).

Whannel, G. (1991) Armchair theatre in the age of fitness chic. In *Social Scientific Perspectives on Sport* (ed. F. Kew), National Coaching Foundation, Leeds.

Whannel, G. (1993) *Television and Sport,* Routledge, London.

White, A. and Brackenridge, C. (1985) Who rules sport? Gender divisions in the power structure of British Sports Organisations from 1960. *International Review for Sociology of Sports,* **20**, 95–107.

White, A., Mayglothling, R. and Carr, C. (1990) *Women sports coaches: a qualitative analysis of role definitions and conflict. XII World Congress of Sociology,* 9–13 July, Madrid.

Whitson, D. (1986) Structure, agency, and the sociology of sport debates. *Theory, Culture and Society,* **3**(1), 99–107.

Whitson, D. and McIntosh, D. (1989) Gender and power. *International Review for Sociology of Sport,* **24**(2), 137–149.

Wilkinson, S. (1990) Stacking in Rugby League, BA dissert. Bradford and Ilkley College (unpublished).

Williams, J. (1994) *Hooligans Abroad,* Routledge and Kegan Paul, London.

Williams, J. (1995) Localism, Globalisation and English Football: The Case of BSkyB. In *Sport in Space and Time* (eds O. Weiss and W. Schulz), University of Vienna Press, Vienna.

Yorganci, I. (1992) Preliminary findings from a survey of gender relationships and sexual harassment in sport. In *Body Matters: Leisure Images and Lifestyles* (ed. C. Brackenridge), Leisure Studies Association, Brighton.

Young, I, (1990) *Throwing Like a Girl and Other Essays in Philosophy and Social Theory*, Indiana University Press, Bloomington.

Young, M. and Wilmott, P. (1973) *The Symmetrical Family*, Routledge and Kegan Paul, London.

Further reading

Bennett, O. (1996) The spectator's guide to sporting snobbery. *The Independent on Sunday*, 21 July.

Bishop, L. (1995) Match points. *Marketing*, 9 Nov, 21–22.

Brackenridge, C. (1994) Fair play or fair game? Child sexual abuse in sport organisations. *International Review for Sociology of Sport*, **29**(3) 287–299.

Bramham, P. (1990) Unsporting youth: sport and youth lifestyles. In *Social Scientific Perspectives on Sport* (ed. F. Kew), Monograph no. 2, British Association of Sports Science, Leeds.

British Institute of Coaches (1989) *Code of Ethics and Code of Conduct*, BIC, Leeds.

Carrington, B., Chivers, T. and Williams, T. (1987) Gender, leisure, and sport: a case-study of young people of South Asian descent. *Leisure Studies*, **6**, 265–279.

Carrington, B. and Leamon, O. (1986) Equal opportunities and physical education. In *Physical Education, Sport and Schooling* (ed. J. Evans), Falmer Press, Lewes, Sussex.

Carroll, B. (1992) Sporting bodies, sporting opportunities: equal opportunity policies in sport and leisure with special reference to ethnic minorities. *Leisure Studies Annual Conference*, Sheffield.

Cashmore, E. (1990) The race season. *New Statesman and New Society*, 1 June, 16–17.

Clement, J.-P. (1995) Contributions of the Sociology of Pierre Bourdieu to the Sociology of Sport. *Sociology of Sport Journal*, **12**, 147–157.

Defrance, J. (1995) The anthropological sociology of Pierre Bourdieu: genesis, concepts, relevance. *Sociology of Sport Journal*, **12**, 121–131.

Gerber, E. (ed.) (1982) *Sport and the Body*, Lea and Febiger, Philadelphia.

Gratton, C. and Nichols, G. (1996) The characteristics of volunteers in UK sports clubs, *World Leisure and Recreation Conference*, Cardiff, 15–19 July.

Gratton, C. and Tice, A. (1994) Trends in sports participation in Britain 1977–87. *Leisure Studies*, **13**, 49–66.

Hall, A. (1985) How should we theorize sport in a capitalist patriarchy. *International Review of Sociology of Sport*, **20**(1–2), 109–116.

Hargreaves, Jen. (ed.) (1982) *Sport, Culture and Ideology*, RKP, London.

Horne, J., Jary, D. and Tomlinson, A. (eds) (1987) *Sport, Leisure and Social Relations*, Routledge and Kegan Paul, London.

Kew, F. (ed.) (1991) *Social Scientific Perspectives on Sport*, National Coaching Foundation, Leeds.

Laberge, S. (1995) Toward an integration of gender into Bourdieu's concept of cultural capital. *Sociology of Sport Journal*, **12**, 132–146.

Lawrence, G. and Rowe, D. (1986) *Power Play: The Commercialisation of Australian Sport*, Hale and Iremonger, Sydney, NSW.

Murphy, M. and White, R. (1978) *The Psychic Side of Sport*, Addison-Wesley, Reading, Massachusetts.

National Coaching Foundation (1995) *Protecting Children: A Guide for Sportspeople*, National Coaching Foundation, Leeds.

Nelson, M. (1996) *The Stronger Women Get, the More Men Love Football: Sexism and the Culture of Sport*, The Women's Press, London.

Nugent, N. and King, R. (1979) Ethnic minorities, scapegoating, and the extreme right. In *Racism and Political Action in Britain* (eds R. Miles and A. Phizacklea), Routledge and Kegan Paul, London.

Roberts, K. (1995) *Leisure and Social Stratification*, pubn. no. 53, Leisure Studies Association, University of Brighton, Eastbourne.

Roberts, K. and Parsell, G. (1994) Youth cultures in Britain: the middle class take over. *Leisure Studies*, **13**, 33–48.

Shaw, G. (1972) *Meat on the Hoof*, St Martin's Press, New York.

Wearing, B. (1995) Leisure and resistance in an ageing society. *Leisure Studies*, **14**(4), 263–280.

Weiss, O. and Schulz, W. (eds) (1995) *Sport in Space and Time*, University of Vienna Press, Vienna.

West, A. and Brockenridge, C. (1990) Wot! No women coaches: a report on the issues relating to women's lives as sports coaches in the UK 1989–90. PAVIC, Sheffield City Polytechnic.

Whannel, G. (1983) *Blowing the Whistle: The Politics of Sport*, Pluto, London.

White, A., Mayglothling, R. and Carr, C. (1989) *The Dedicated Few: The Social World of Women Coaches in Britain in the 1980's*, West Sussex Institute of HE, Chichester.

Whitson, D. (1977) Autonomy, play and sport. *Journal of Psychosocial Aspects of Human Movement*, no. 3, Dunfermline College.

Index

Accessibility of sport, 111–14
Adapted sports, 114–16
Afro-caribbeans, 90–100
Agency and structure, 79–82, 83
Amateurism, 1, 24–26
Asians in sport, 101–5

Biologism, 93
Blood-doping, 68
British Institute of Sports Coaches, 77
British Sports Association for the Disabled, 110, 115
British Olympic Association, 38, 68
Bureaucratization, 15, 17
Burn-out, 72, 77–8

Cable television, 53–4
Capital, 33
 cultural capital, 150–2
 political capital, 79
Central Council for Physical Recreation, 66–7
Channelling into sport, 95–6
Class consciousness, 143
Coaching, 55, 100
 abuse, 69–73
 women, 135–7

Codes of Conduct, 77
Commerce, 30, 41–3, 53
Commodification, 32–55, 80
Community recreation, 104–6, 142

Disability, 108
Disablism, 109
Disassociation from sport, 59, 67
Drugs in sport, 8, 68, 78

Elite athletes, 52, 54, 78
Ethics in sport, 56–7, 78
Ethnicity, 88
Ethnocentrism, 88, 106
Equal opportunities, 124, 140
Equality, 15–16, 122, 138
Equity in sport, 122, 137
Exploitation of athletes, 68–78, 81, 139

Fair play, 43, 46–47, 56–7, 58, 66
Feminism, 13, 30–1, 134, 139–42
Flow experience, 11
Funnelling into sport, 101

Gender, 124, 126
Globalization processes, 49–51

Heritage events, 41, 47

Impairment, 108
Individualism, 83
Institute of Child Health, 76
Institute of Sports Sponsorship, 39
International Management Group, 38
Integration into sport, 118–20
Internal goods of sport, 8, 10–11, 79
Instrumentalization of sport, 20, 58, 80, 152

Marketing, 38
Match-fixing, 72
Multi-culturalism, 88

New Games, 142
National Coaching Foundation, 77, 136
National Governing Bodies, 27–31, 34, 62
National Lottery, 27

Olympics, 38, 41, 63, 65, 80, 93, 119
Outdoor activities, 31
Over-training, 72, 74

Paradox of sport, 5
Paralympics, 119
Physical education, 20, 103, 116–18, 128, 130–2, 137
Play:
  concept of, 5
  duality of, 7
Players associations, 54
Professional Footballers Association, 54
Professionalism, 21, 24–6, 55
Profile system, 119–21

Quantification of sport, 15, 18

Race, 89
Racism, 89–90, 106, 139
Rationalization of sport, 15, 17, 20
Records in sport, 15, 18
Rules of sport:
  changes, 21–2, 43–5, 64–5
  letter and spirit, 60–2
  violations, 62–3, 79

Scottish Sports Council, 112–13
Secularism, 15–16
Sex discrimination, 124
Sexism in sport, 127, 139
Sexual harassment in sport, 69–71
Sexuality and sport, 134–5
Sex-role, 127, 136

Social class and sport,
143–60
Social divisions, 84
Social dynamics of sport,
8–10
Social policy and sport,
105–7, 159–60
Social structure, 84
Social surveys, 144
Socialization, 128–32
Specialization, 128–32
Spectacularization of
sport, 15–16, 47–9
Spending on sport, 35
Sports Aid Foundation,
38, 52
Sports Council, 26, 33,
35, 68, 76, 87, 102,
110, 125, 136, 146,
147, 157
Sportsmatch, 39
Sport, concept of:
association, 23–4, 58
institution of, 3, 7,
11–13
social practice of, 3, 7,
19

Sports worlds, 19, 22–7
Stacking in sport,
98–100
Stereotyping, 85, 101–2,
106, 133, 139
Stock market, sports
investments in, 53

Trash sports, 48
Television and sport, 22,
36, 40–3, 45, 47–9,
53, 132

Underclass, 157–8

Values in sport, ix, 56
Value-judgements, 1–3,
56
Vertical segregation,
136

Women and media sport,
54, 128, 132–3
World Series Cricket, 45

Youth sport, 55, 69,
76–7, 104